CROCHET FOR BEGINNERS

IF YOU DECIDED TO LEARN HOW TO CROCHET AND DON'T KNOW WHERE TO START, HERE IS A SIMPLE BEGINNER'S GUIDE WITH PATTERNS AND TIPS, AND CREATIVE CHALLENGES FOR EXPERTS.

Table of Contents

Introduction 1

Chapter 1   How to read and understand crochet 8

Why Crochet As A Hobby...8

Chapter 2   Tools and materials 11

Yarn 11

Choosing the Best Yarn for Crochet 11

Additional Yarn Tips and Considerations................................. 13

Hooks 14

Types of Crochet Hooks 16

Tools You Need for Crocheting.. 19

Chapter 3   Hook and yarn 26

Holding the Hook 26

All About Yarn 28

Chapter 4   Crochet Tips and Tricks.................................... 32

Mistakes Crochets Make and Solution......................................35

Chapter 5   Learn the basic steps step by step 42

Lesson 1: How to Hold the Crochet Hook................................42

Lesson 2: How to Slip Knot and Chain Stitch..........................46

Lesson 3: How to Single Crochet 51

Lesson 4: How to Half Double Crochet.....................................57

Lesson 5: How to Treble Crochet 60

Lesson 6: How to Crochet a Turning chain 65

Lesson 7: How to Join Yarn...66

Lesson 8: How to Crochet in the Front and Back loop 67

Lesson 9: Fastening Off 69

Chapter 6   Patterns and explanations: **70**

Understanding Pattern 70

How To Read A Crochet Pattern? 72

Circle Patterns 73

Working With A Hole As A Center Ring 73

Working Into The Chain Stitch 74

Abbreviations 77

Chapter 7   For Beginners **79**

How To Read Stitch Patterns 79

Lightweight Textured Stitch Patterns 86

Chapter 8   For Advanced **90**

Pineapple Lace 90

Bullion Stitch 90

Loop Stitch 91

Crocodile Stitch 91

Starting and finishing project 91

Chapter 9   Patterns and Explanations for Children **95**

Wrist Warmers 95

Baby Blanket 97

Perfect Pillows 97

Miniature Hat Ornament 97

Tunisian Scarf 99

Faux Knit Headband 100

Tunisian Crochet Cellphone Bag 102

Tunisian Stitch Neck Warmer 103

Afghan Stitch Coaster...105

One Skein Scarf...106

Chapter 10 Tunisian crochet **107**

Getting Started...110

The Foundational Row And The Forward Pass............................110

Knit Stitches And The Forward Pass...113

Finishing or Binding..115

Basic Tunisian Crochet Stitches 116

Chapter 11 Crochet mandala **124**

Sample of Most Gorgeous Patterns with Easy Instructions 124

Pattern 01: Blooming Mandala...124

Pattern 02: Flower Madala 131

Chapter 12 Techniques and Stitches....................................**133**

Techniques...133

Stitches..144

Making different shapes...147

Chapter 13 Choosing a Crochet Pattern **153**

Different Types Of Yarns You Can Find, And You May Use In Your

Crochet 154

How Social Media Can Help You With Your Crochet Patterns 155

Considering The Proper Way Of Holding The Crochet Needle 155

Common Crochet Designs 156

Chapter 14 Crocheting Background.....................................**163**

What makes one think of crocheting?..164

The Economic part of Crocheting...167

Social and Traditional Impact of Crocheting..............................168

Chapter 15   Benefits of Crocheting................................**172**

Chapter 16   History of Crochet **175**

    Crocheted Projects 178

    Early Origins and History...................................... 180

Chapter 17   Glossary **185**

    Abbreviations 185

    Terms 185

    How to Read Crochet Patterns and Terminology 187

    Common Crochet Terminology and Abbreviations..................... 188

    Crochet Terms Used in UK and US 189

Chapter 18   FAQ's About Yarn Care **192**

    Can You Wash An Entire Skein?.................................. 192

    How Often Should You Wash Yarn Or Wool?.......................... 193

    Can You Dye Your Own Yarn? 193

    How Do You Find Yarn Care Instructions For Other Yarn? 193

    Can You Get Rid Of Old Stains And Smells?....................... 194

    Can You Tumble Dry?... 194

    How Long Can You Keep Yarn Or Wool For? 194

    How Do You Store Yarn?..195

Conclusions **196**

Introduction

Crochet is an embroidery method that utilizes a crochet hook with fiber or similar material. This fiber is most usually wool or crochet thread, but it could also be leather, rope, twine, or other inventive content.

Crochet fans are looking forward to finishing crochet creations that are usually useful, desirable, or helpful items in some way. Common initiatives typically involve Afghans, crocheted blankets, baby booties, sweaters, beanies, and squares of granny, shawls, pouches, tote bags, and many others. A number of different things can be crocheted, including brooches, socks, and curtains.

It is also important to use different components in other products to crochet. Crochet trims as well as edgings, for example, are common projects; you may add them to crocheted products, knitted items, as well as sewn pieces (including ready-made shop-bought items), such as purchasing some shoes, towels, and/or pillow cases, and applying a crocheted finish to each.

Studies shows that crochet was actually more specifically derived from Chinese needlework, a very ancient form of embroidery found in Turkey, India, Persia, and North Africa that entered Europe in the 1700s and was referred to as "tambouring," from those in the French "tambour" or drum. A backdrop cloth is placed on a plate in this technique.

Under the cloth is kept the working yarn. A needle with a hook is inserted downwards, and through the fabric, a loop of the working thread is drawn. The hook is then inserted a little further along with the loop still on the hook, and then another loop of that same working thread is taken up and waited to form a chain stitch thru the first loop.

The hooks of the tambour were as thin as needles of sewing, so the work had to be done with really fine thread.

Tambour developed in to what the French termed "crochet in the air" at the end of the 18th century when the fabric of the background was discarded, and the stitch worked alone.

In the early 1800s, crochet started to appear by Europe and was offered a massive boost by Mlle. Riego de la Branchardiere, who has been best remembered for her ability to make crochet variations that could readily be duplicated by taking old-style needle as well as bobbin lace styles.

She authored many trend books in order to start copying her designs by millions of women. Miss. Riego also helped popularize "lace-like" crochet, also named Irish crochet. Irish crochet was a practical lifesaver for the citizens of Ireland.

This lifted them off of their potato famine, which persisted from 1845 to 1850 and plunged them into abject poverty. In those days, comfortable living standards for the Irish were severe.

A wide range of fabrics have been used across the ages: feathers, grasses, reeds, horse hair and sinew, corn, flax, leather, gold and silver and copper fibers, silk, woolen thread, wool yarns (soft zephyr yam, luster yarn, double cable yarn, carpet yarn), cotton yarns (anchor and estramadura), silk threads (cordonnet and floss), linen strings, hemp threads, mohair, chenille, modern mixtures, meta combinations.

We now have a huge selection of linen, wool, silk as well as organic yarns at our fingertips. With these uncommon materials such as copper cable, plastic strips, sisal, jute, fabric scraps, unspun wool, and sometimes even dog hair, we could also crochet.

And what about the device for crochet? We are now going into a yarn shop or Costco and purchasing metal, plastic, or steel hooks in over 25 size options.

Though, in ancient times, they used everything they could get their hands on-first fingers, after which hooks made from metal, wood, fishbone, animal bone, horn, old spoons, teeth of thrown away combs, brass, mother-of-pearl, morse, tortoiseshell, ivory, copper, steel, vulcanite, ebonite, silver as well as agate.

In Dublin at the period of the great purge (1845 to 1850), that at least one individual used to make fine Irish crochet was indeed a needle or a steep wire threaded into a cork or slice of timber or tree bark, with both the end filed down and twisted into a tiny loop.

Person-and it was the men's role-created his craftsmanship for practical reasons in the early centuries. To catching animals as well as snare fish or birds, hunters, as well as fishermen, produced knotted chains of twisted fabrics, cords, or strips of fabric. Other implementations included braided game bags, fishing nets as well as kitchen utensils that were open-worked.

To important occasions like those of religious ceremonies, holidays, weddings, or funerals, handwork has been extended to include informal decoration. In crochet-like adornments and ornamental drippings for arms, ankles as well as wrists, most of us see ceremonial outfits.

In Europe of the 16th century, aristocracy and the wealthy were adorned in gold trimmings, gowns, hats, headpieces-and the poor folk would only hope of wearing these items. And, it's thought, crochet was created as the emulation of the lace of the rich man by the poor people.

Continuing into the Victorian era, crochet designs were popular for flowerpot holders, bird cage covers, visiting card frames, lamp mats and shades, wastepaper containers, tablecloths, antimacassars (or "antis," covers to shield chairbacks from hair oil worn by men in the mid-1800s), cigarette packs, purses, men's caps, and waistcoats, even a footwarming rug to be put undead.

People were also busy crocheting Afghans from 1900 to 1930, sleeping rugs, walking rugs, chaise lounge, sleigh rugs, vehicle rugs, cushions, coffee and teapot cozies, and hot water bottle coverings. During this period, potholders rendered their first appearances and then became a standard of the arsenal of that same crocheter.

Then, of course, there is something going on. Crochet started off as an impressionistic medium of communication in the 1960s and 1970s that can now be seen in three-dimensional paintings, textile pieces, or rugs and tapestries portraying abstract and practical patterns and scenes.

Comparing crochet techniques from the past against those we employ today is fascinating. For illustration, it is recorded in the Dutch journal, Penelope, during the period 1824 to 1833 that both the yarn and the hook had to be kept in the hand while holding and the yarn moved from the right forefinger over the hook.

The thread is kept in the right hand as well as the wool in the left in crochet textbooks from the 1840s, as right-handers do now.

In a German publishing dated 1847, it indicated that you should "keep the very same tightness, either crochet crudely or crochet tightly, otherwise you won't achieve an attractive even texture. Moreover, if you don't work on the round, you need to split off your yarn at just the end of each row, as this provides the crocheted item a finer finish." At the flip of the 20th century, this change occurred.

Researcher Lis Paludan theorizes that perhaps the exhortation to retain the same tension "seems to mean that crochet needles are all of the same width and that the crocheter was required to work in the right tension according to fashion."

Ancient design directions, dating back to the mid-1800s, suggested that the hook was only to be used in the second half of the stitch using a single crochet stich.

Jenny Lambert, a German, wrote in 1847 that putting the sole crochet in the back half of that same stitching was useful to make table runners and so on, but running the hook through those loops could be used to "crochet sole for shoes and other things that must be thicker than normal, but the procedure is not ideal for designs."

Another simply copied the work of someone else until ideas were recorded. Specimens were made, sewn and attached like scrapbooks, stitched on large strips of fabric, or left loose in a bag or case. Writer Annie Potter discovered many of these scrapbooks in use by nuns in Spain in her travels, dating back to the late 1800s.

A further way of collecting stitch patterns was to knit various stitches in large, thin bands together-some created by parents, some begun at school then added to it over the years. (Subsequently, in Europe, around 1916 to around 1926, readers were able to buy tiny pattern variations together with their yarn.) In 1824, the first crochet patterns documented to date were printed.

The first designs of color work crochet were for silver and gold silk thread purses.

In many nations, crochet books have been discovered, mostly translated from one language into another. Mlle was perhaps the most popular crochet specialist. Riego de la Branchardiere, who has written over a 100 novels, has released many on crochet.

The crochet publications from the mid-1800s were slim but also included woodcut drawings, only around 4 inches by 6 inches. According to Paludan, these tiny gems included designs for white buttons-like collars, cuffs, lace, insertions including caps for women and kids, along with models for handbags, slippers, and hats for men.

Cotton thread, coil yarn (Scottish thread on spools), linen, or hemp thread is preferred fabrics for white crochet (insertions, edgings, pads, underwear trimming). Silk, wool as well as chenille yarns were recommended for colorwork and also precious metals threads.

Such early designs would make current crocheters nuts, many of which were not correct. For example, an eight-pointed star could turn out to have only six points. It transforms out that the reader was required to read the sequence and to use the depiction as the most precise guide.

Chapter 1 How to read and understand crochet

Crocheting is simply the process of creating fabric by intertwining loops of thread, yarn wire, twine or strands of other types of innovative material using a crochet hook. The name 'crochet' is derived from a French word 'croche', which literally translates to hook. In French, crochet means small hook. The hooks used in crocheting are usually made of materials such as plastic, wood or metal.

Why Crochet As A Hobby

Among all the hobbies there are, why bother with crocheting? Well, let us find out:

1. Crocheting can Reduces Stress and Anxiety

When you crochet, you need to be in the moment and concentrate on your work or you will end up messing everything, which can be a lot of work trying to undo. This ability to be in the moment working on something enables you not to have too many thoughts racing through your mind. Your mind is able to free itself from anxious ideas or thoughts and be more relaxed when you focus on counting rows, and the repetitive motions of individual stitches.

2. Helps Relieve or Ease Depression

Whenever we do something that we like or enjoy, our brain releases a chemical known as dopamine, which affects emotions like a natural anti-depressant. According to scientists, crafts such as crocheting may help in stimulating the release of dopamine thereby allowing you to feel happier. Furthermore, you derive great satisfaction when you see the progress in your work and when you finally finish a project, which makes you feel great about yourself.

3. Helps with Insomnia

When you focus your mind on something that is easy, soothing and repetitive such as crochet, it helps in calming your mind and body enough to allow you to fall asleep. Therefore, the next time you are having a hard time getting some sleep, don't get frustrated, just pick up your tools and crochet and before long, you will feel sleepy.

4. Builds your Self-Esteem

We all want to feel useful and productive and by working on a crochet project to sell at a craft fair or give as a gift, we can just do that. This does not necessarily mean that we crochet to fish for compliments, however, a little external validation by your gift recipient wearing the scarf or mittens you made through winter or someone buying your finished item can give you the boost of self-esteem that you need.

5. Crocheting Reduces the Risk of Alzheimer's by 30-50%

By stimulating your mind and engaging in cognitive exercises, you can slow down or prevent memory loss. Whether you are challenging your memory by simply reading, trying out a pattern or learning a new technique or stitch, getting a little crafty helps you to preserve your memory.

6. Crocheting Puts You in Control

Whether you are feeling helpless watching someone struggle or you are the one struggling with your own problems or illness, crocheting is a great way to put back the control into your hands - literally. When you chose to create, you are in full control of everything, from the project type, the type of crochet hooks and even the type and color of yarn you will be using. This makes all the difference in the world, as it makes you feel like you finally have a say.

7. Crocheting Acts as a Form of Group Therapy

Working on a project in a group helps those in the group to have an immediate way of relating to the other group members and can work as an ice breaker for more serious discussions or conversations. Even if you are not seeking therapy actively, you can enjoy the sense of community brought about by crocheting.

Chapter 2 Tools and materials

Basics: You only need yarn/thread, crochet hooks and scissors to start crocheting.

Yarn

You can use a variety of yarns to crochet but the type of yarn you chose depends on the type of project. You can crochet with any kind of yarn, even non-fiber yarn-like materials. While you can use any type of yarn, as a beginner, you will find it best to use the yarn options we will outline below since they are easier to work with than others are.

Choosing the Best Yarn for Crochet

1. Fiber type

This is the first decision you have to make as you embark on your crochet journey. There are quite a number of options to choose from for both plant and animal fibres. However, we will focus on the three most common and basic ones: acrylic, cotton and wool.

You might be wondering how to know which type of fiber you are working with but it's really quite simple – the type of fiber is usually listed on the yarn label. Although as you familiarize yourself with crocheting, you will find yourself being able to identify the fiber type by just handling or even looking at the yarn.

2. **Acrylic yarn**: Acrylic is generally a popular yarn among crochet enthusiasts. It is usually among the affordable choices for yarn, comes in a variety of colors and is widely available. It is a more-than-acceptable choice for you as a beginner. However, you should be aware that some of the cheapest acrylics split apart thereby making it quite challenging to work with. This case is not usually common but it does happen. Therefore, if you are having a hard time working with acrylic, try switching to a different brand or you can just use wool or cotton instead.

3. **Cotton yarn**: It's an inelastic fiber thereby making it a bit more challenging to work with than wool. However, where you want the item to hold its shape, this quality makes cotton a great choice for specific projects. Although some may find it a bit more challenging than wool, it is not that different at all and it is something you can certainly try as a beginner. If you are crocheting during summer where working with wool is unpleasant due to the heat, cotton is a great choice since its lighter than wool.

4. **Wool Yarn**: Wool is the perfect choice for you to practice your stitches. It is forgiving of mistakes and is a resilient fiber. If you happen to make a mistake while crocheting, most wool yarns, are easy to unravel and even re-use (in crochet, it's called frogging). Wool yarn is not suitable for those with wool allergies but for most, it is a good crocheting choice.

Additional Yarn Tips and Considerations

1. **Yarn weight***:* Yarns come in different thicknesses as well. This thickness is what we refer to as weight. The weight of the yarn is usually found on the label where it's numbered 1-7 (from the thinnest to the thickest). It is easiest to work with a worsted weight yarn as a beginner, which is #4 on the yarn label.

***Note:** it is advisable that you use the correct crochet hook size for the yarn weight you will be using.

2. **Yarn color***:* Choose lighter yarn colors rather than dark ones, as it can get challenging to see your stitches if using yarns with dark colors.

3. **Yarn texture***:* Choose smooth yarn and not the textured ones. As you begin crocheting, avoid eyelash yarns and any other textured novelty yarns, which can get quite frustrating to work with.

4. **Yarn yardage***:* Each ball of yarn has different yardage amounts, which relates to the price. You can find 2 balls of yarn with the same price; just check the yardage to ensure the amount of yarn in each ball is approximately the same.

5. **Yarn price***:* The price of yarn varies significantly from brand to brand and fiber to fiber. It is better to work on the affordable ones so that you get the hang of it before investing a lot of money in very expensive yarns. This is

why acrylic, wool and cotton are the top fiber choices, as they tend to be the most affordable.

6. **Yarn color dye lot**: If you want to crochet a large project that will need more than 1 ball of yarn, then you want to ensure that all the colors match (assuming that you are using the same color-way or color for the entire project). You do this by checking the "dye lot on the yarn label to ensure that the balls are from the same dye lot number so that they don't have noticeable differences between them.

7. **Washing details**: Different fiber types have different washing instructions, which will be really important if you are crocheting something to wear. For instance, you can use superwash wool that is safe to put in the washer and dryer or you can go so for some type of wool that must be hand washed and dried flat because it will shrink in the dryer. The yarn label contains this information to aid in your selections.

Hooks

The average crochet hook works for anyone and it definitely favours beginners like you. You will find crochet hooks sold at yarn stores or any major craft retailer. You can also get them online. Below are a few things you need to know about crochet hooks:

1. **Material**: A basic crochet hook can be made of several common materials such as bamboo, plastic and aluminum. Most people usually choose aluminum crochet hooks for their first project. There are also fancier crochet hooks made of wood, glass, and clay.

2. **Size**: Crochet hooks differ in size; there are many different sizes which are measured in numbers, letters or millimetres. For instance, a basic crochet hook set may range from E – J. A general-sized crochet hook is normally H-8 5mm. Size E is smaller than size H, size J is larger. As mentioned, you should match the size of your crochet hook with the weight of your yarn, which is usually on the label of the yarn. For most beginners, it is usually advisable to work with a size G or H crochet hook and worsted weight yarn.

3. **Hook throat**: A crochet hook has either an inline or tapered "throat", resulting in less or more flatness to the head of the hook. Since neither is better than the other is, if you find it hard to work with one, just try the other.

Types of Crochet Hooks

Let us now look at the various types of crochet hooks at your disposal as you get started:

1. Thread Crochet Hooks

When you are using thread to crochet instead of yarn, the crochet hook you use is similar but it is quite smaller than a yarn hook. The hooks are also usually made of steel in order to prevent bending while you crochet, a problem that is less popular among larger hook sizes.

2. Light-up crochet hooks

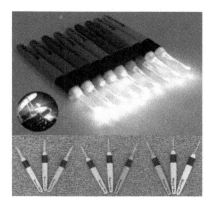

If you suffer from insomnia or if you simply want to crochet in the middle of the night without being a bother to anyone, then light-up crochet hooks are what you need.

They light up at the tip so that it is easier to see where you are going to insert the hook to crochet. They are typically regular crochet hooks that light up.

3. Ergonomic crochet hooks

Sometimes it can become quite uncomfortable to crochet with regular hooks for a long time especially if you suffer from hand conditions such as arthritis or carpal tunnel. Fortunately, there are ergonomic crochet hooks, which have larger handles that are shaped to create a grip that makes it easier to crochet for long.

4. Tunisian crochet hooks

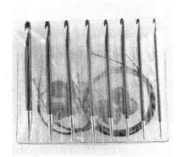

Tunisian crochet is a niche of crocheting that uses a completely different set of stitches from regular crocheting. Tunisian crochet hooks are also known as Afghan crochet hooks and are longer than the regular crochet hooks. These hooks can have a cable to connect a one-headed hook to another one-headed hook or they can have a head on either side of the hook.

5. Knook

A knook looks like a regular crochet hook but it has a small hole drilled into one end where you insert the thread for holding your stitches.

Tools You Need for Crocheting

Crocheting is easy and fun! However, one needs the right equipment to complete a project successfully. The following tools are essential in crocheting projects:

1. **Hook:** This is used to make loops and interlock them into stitches. Hooks are composed of steel, plastic, aluminum, bone, tortoiseshell, or wood, among other materials. It is upon the individual to choose a comfortable hook. However, that choice is largely determined by the size of yarn and the holes that one wants, as well as the instructions specified in the pattern.

Hooks come in varying sizes, designs, and thickness. It is imperative to note that a larger hook would be used with thicker yarns, whereas a smaller hook is used with fine threads.

When first starting with crocheting, a good choice is to start with I/9-5.50mm aluminum hook. It is very comfortable for beginners because it is light and yarn grips to it very well while creating bigger stitches that are easier to see.

2. **Scissors:** They are used to cut the yarn after finishing a garment or sewing seams together. A small pair of blunt-end scissors in good condition is suitable for a crochet project.

3. **Flexible tape measure:** Used to measure the length and width of a garment to establish the gauge required by the pattern. A flexible tape measure is good for measuring both straight and round rows.

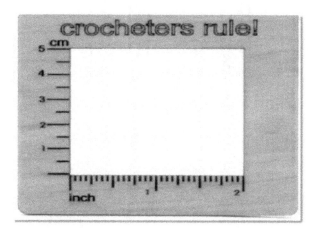

4. **Gauge Ruler:** This is a 2-inch L shaped window item used to measure the number of rows and stitches in an inch.

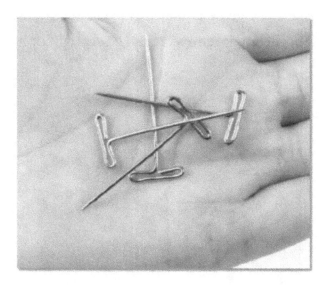

5. **T pins:** These are used to block and secure pieces of the project together when measuring, joining, or blocking.

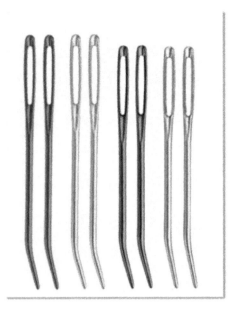

6. **Darning/yarn/tapestry needle:** This tool for hiding loose ends when joining yarn or seams of the completed project. The needle is made of plastic or metal and has a blunt point and large eye. It can be straight or have a slight bend.

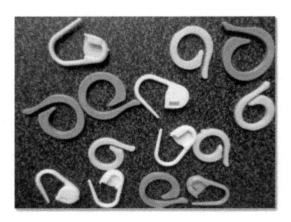

7. **Stitch markers:** These are devices that slip into a garment to show a certain point such as joining continuous rounds, increase points, or decrease points. They show where a stitch begins or ends, thereby keeping one on track. They come in different colors to make work easier.

8. **Pencil and a small note pad:** These are used to keep track of the row or round that one is crocheting or the number of times stitches have been repeated. They are also useful for writing small notes about each project.

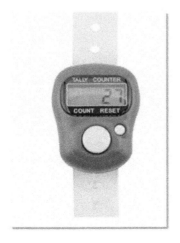

9. **Digital row counter:** This tool helps one keep track of crocheting work such as the number of rounds made or rows completed, which in turn, saves a lot of time.

10. **Crochet tool organizer:** This picture is an example of a useful crochet tool organizer that holds a hook organizer, scissors, and tape measures, among other crocheting equipment. You can make a crochet tool organizer or buy one from various shops.

11. **Blocking surface:** Every crocheter needs a good surface for blocking crochet pieces. Any flat, soft surface such as a bed would suffice, but a more suitable blocking surface would be a board or a mat as pictured here.

Chapter 3 Hook and yarn

Holding the Hook

There is no hard and fast rule for holding the hook and yarn. The rule of thumb is to choose the method you find most comfortable. Some people use the "pencil grip" where the hook is held like a pencil.

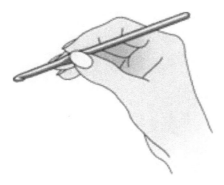

Others use the "knife grip" by holding the hook like a dinner knife that is ready to cut.

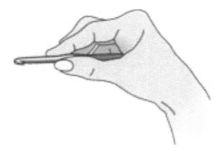

Be sure to maintain a slight tension in the yarn for easy and even stitches. Wrap the yarn around a finger of the hand opposite the one holding the hook as shown below.

In the picture below, the left hand not only holds the crochet work but also controls the tension of the yarn. The middle finger manipulates the yarn, while the index finger and thumb hold the project.

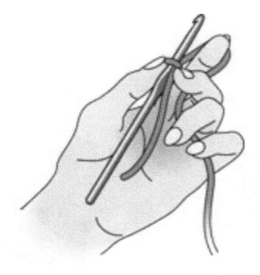

Some people manipulate the yarn with the index finger and hold the crochet work with thumb and middle finger, as shown below.

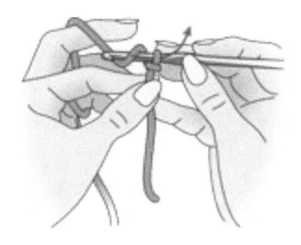

Feel free to try different techniques until you find one that is comfortable for you.

All About Yarn

Selecting Yarn

Crochet yarns are constructed of natural fibers like cotton, linen, wool, or silk, or synthetic fibers such as polyester or acrylic. Yarns are available in different weights and fiber contents.

When purchasing yarn, you should consider your allergies and sensitivities, the thread's stickiness, breathability, and whether or not it is machine washable. When buying yarn for any project, follow these simple guidelines:

Be on the lookout for quality yarn because it affects the appearance of the finished project. Good quality yarn has the following characteristics. The yarn will have a firm twist so as not to separate easily when crocheting, as well as an even thickness, to ensure equal stitches in the garment. The yarn will have a consistent texture, with an even color throughout the skein, and good resiliency. Resiliency means the yarn easily springs back in place when squeezed or stretched.

Always buy enough yarn to complete a project. Buy thread with matching colors, as well as dye lots. Buy all the yarn you will need at one time to ensure you get the same dye lot. This way, every ball of thread will be precisely the same color. It's always a good practice to buy extra yarn if you are not sure of the amount needed to complete a garment.

It is imperative to use the type of yarn specified in the pattern instructions. There are pattern instructions that indicate a particular type of yarn. Sometimes, you can use a yarn conversion chart to substitute a different yarn. However, in such a case, the substitute thread should meet the gauge given in the instructions.

Follow the right blocking procedures for every type of thread chosen to complete a project. Blocking is a process used to shape crocheted work. The fiber content of the thread determines the blocking method. Moreover, it is advisable to read the yarn label to understand the blocking instructions.

Yarn Color

To get the best out of any yarn color, always choose and coordinate hues or colors with intensities that look good when combined. When you choose a brighter intensity, you will need a complementary color.

For instance, bright pink (bright intensity) combines well with dusty rose (dull intensity) and leaf green (semi-dull intensity).

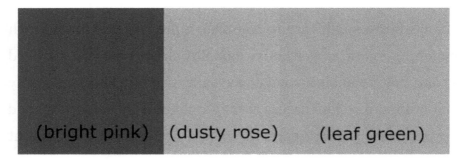

(bright pink) (dusty rose) (leaf green)

Choose five (or less) colors for one project. The recommended guide is one to three color choices depending on the item created and its function. Note that it is better to have an odd number of colors rather than an even number in a single project. Vary the number of colors in a project, but have one color hue as the main color. This variation makes a project more interesting.

Generally, black, gray, and white are considered neutral colors and as such, can be used without upsetting the color formula of a color scheme. In most cases, black and white are utilized as accent colors.

Generally, beginners should start with a thick yarn of solid bright or light color. Using brighter colors helps to distinguish stitches as compared to using a dark or multicolored yarn, which may make it difficult to pinpoint stitches. Furthermore, beginners should use medium, worsted weight thread made of wool or acrylic fibers.

Yarn Label

Read the yarn label carefully to make sure you are buying the correct yarn for a project. Check the dye lot numbers because a slight difference in the color may not be noticeable until you have completed the project.

Keep the yarn label even after you have used the yarn because it shows you how to take care of your item after it is complete.

Chapter 4 Crochet Tips and Tricks

1. To avoid balls of yarn from falling and rolling, place them in reused hand wipe jar of cylindrical shape. Just like wipes, the yarn will also come out through the same hole.

2. Mark your rows by using a stitch marker, bobby pin, safety pin.

3. Store your crochet hooks in the jewelry box, pencil box or travelling toothpaste holder. You can also hang your hooks on a small piece of wool. A multipurpose storage box is also a good option.

4. Highlight your pattern with different colors so that you can understand it easily. Underline different stitches. If your patterns demand rows of different color, highlight the rows with the same color or with the colors that you have decided to use.

5. Always keep abbreviations, measurements, hook and yarn weights table in printable forms so that you can easily use them whenever you want.

6. Use rapped or leftover yarns to make pom poms, Afghan squares, bracelets and many more articles like these.

7. If you use the homespun yarn for your pattern, then metal hooks are a better option than plastic ones.

8. If you love to do crochet during travelling, prepare a separate crochet box. Always have travel-friendly crochet tools, for example, foldable scissors that are easy to carry and also will not snug the things in the bag.

9. Many crochet patterns do not go well with ironing. So instead of it, take an equal quantity of water and starch and spray the pattern with it and let it dry on a flat surface.

10. Store the crochet patterns in your notebook by using sheet protectors.

11. Make sure you sit in proper position to provide enough support to your elbows, and hands during crocheting.

12. Take breaks after regular intervals to refresh yourself.

13. There are a variety of hand massage and stretching techniques. So do any of them that you find it easy to relax your hand muscles.

14. Using ergonomic crochet tools such as circular needles is also useful to avoid hand fatigue.

15. Use stress relief gloves.

16. Pick up your hook every day. The hardest part about learning how to crochet is training your hand to hold your hook (and the yarn) with the correct tension. At first, it feels a little awkward and unnatural but if you make it a habit of picking up your hook every day when you are first learning the craft; it will become easy in no time. Do not give up and keep in mind that practice makes perfect!

17. Begin with small projects. Learning how to crochet takes time and most of the times, beginners feel discouraged when they are not able to complete a project – I mean, who wouldn't? The best thing to do is to start with small attainable projects. There is no better feeling than completing your very own first project. Start with small items such as squares, mandalas and coasters before moving onto larger projects such as blankets and cushions

18. Chain, chain, chain. When learning to crochet, making several chains is the best way to improve your tension since they are the foundation of all stitches. You will be ready for stitches that are more complicated once all your chains look nice and even

19. Make stitch swatches. You can work on small swatches to help you to familiarize yourself with the different stitches. You can even sew these swatches together to create face cloths or small blankets

20. Avoid Changing Hooks in the Middle of a Project. Your stitches should be consistent throughout the whole project. When you switch hooks mid-project, you risk creating an inconsistency. Even changing same size hooks from one manufacture to another can be problematic. This is because the size of the hook is not always the same between manufacturers and small change in how the hooks are shaped can change the way you create your stitches or hold the hook hence the need of practice swatches.

Mistakes Crochets Make and Solution

As a beginner, you must come across your fair share of frustrations as you get stuck into your crocheting. Mistakes could happen by not following instructions accurately, or simply as a result of practice. Remember, there are certain methods you can adjust slightly to suit you, as long as they don't affect the appearance of your stitches and your pattern.

Learning to crochet can be a wonderful experience, so try not to get too despondent if you don't always manage to do everything properly at first. It is a very time-consuming craft and requires a lot of skill which you will develop over time. Don't be too hard on yourself and just have fun.

Perhaps you may not be familiar with some of these depending on how much crocheting you have done up to this point. Read through them and keep them in mind if you ever have any of these challenges in the future.

1. Inserting your hook into the wrong chain when you start

Don't count the first chain on the hook because it is just a loop, your first proper chain is the first chain from the hook which is the one next to and the one after that is the second loop on the hook.

When you use US stitches when your pattern contains UK pattern terms

This can sometimes be really easy to miss and cause several complications. An easy way to check is to look out for single crochet instruction as this confirms that your pattern is a US pattern that uses US terminology.

2. Not considering blocking as an important step

First of all, blocking involves handwashing an item and then pinning it into place on a blocking mat. The reason for doing this is to straighten the item and flatten it if needed. It is possible to machine wash your item, just use the hand setting. There are times when blocking isn't completely necessary, whereas so for you. If you intend to wash it then be sure to use the blocked gauge measurements.

3. Making starting loops using linked chains and not a magic loop

You could use methods of starting your crocheting in the round. The first is to work four or five chain stitches and join them in a circle by using a slipstitch. This is the simplest method.

However, a more effective method is to start loops using a magic circle. The center of the circle is much tighter than that of a regular circle linked by a chain stitch. The important thing to remember is consistency, if you use motifs on any items, only use one method to create them as your work will be tidier. So, try them both and see which one you are more comfortable with using and stick to that method.

4. Not changing the size of your hook as needed

You may have done this and only realized it when your work didn't look quite right. This can happen when your starting chain is rather tight in comparison to the rest of your work. This is, however, a common mistake among beginners. It is essential that you have the right tension in your chain as it forms the foundation of your work.

One solution is to use a slightly larger hook than recommended in your pattern as this will help you to have a more even tension throughout. It is not necessary to change the size of your hook if your tension is correct. Always be aware of specific crochet hook sizes on your patterns.

5. Your work seems to be shrinking

If you find that your work is shrinking in places and the shape of your item doesn't look right, then you have probably made an error somewhere. The explanation for a mistake such as this is usually a result of making your first stitch in the incorrect position.

Remember these points:

- For a single crochet, the first stitch is inserted into the first stitch of the row above.

- For your other basic stitches, it is the turning chain which is to be counted as the first stitch. Hence, this first stitch is inserted into what is the second one of the previous rows.

6. Not being able to identify your stitches

It is common for beginners to be so involved in trying to follow the instructions in their patterns that they seldom check to see whether their stitches actually look the way they should. Never fear, this is quite normal, and a mistake made by so many of us. There are lots of different moving parts and it takes a while to catch your rhythm. When you first start crocheting, take a moment to count your stitches and learn what they look like.

7. Avoiding new techniques because they seem too difficult.

If something seems too difficult, look at it more carefully before avoiding it completely. If you can do the basic stitches, you'll be able to handle nearly all the crochet techniques without any problem. You may just need to practice a few times. The steps can sometimes seem a bit intimidating, but if you read through them, you'll see that they are made up of basic instructions. So, don't avoid trying something new, it may be easier than you think and you'll be able to take your crochet to a new level before you know it!

8. Not learning enough about yarn

When you start buying yarns, learn as much as you can about them. You will, of course, have to use certain yarns depending on the patterns you are using. But also try and find out which ones are of good quality and don't always go for the cheapest.

You don't realize that your turning chain is the same height as the first stitch in the row.

You should be able to see that the starting chain of your row brings the height of your work up to that of the first stitch in that row. For example, single crochet is one chain and half double crochet is two chains. Have a look at this the next time you are crocheting.

9. Not being able to read patterns

Nowadays, one can tend to be a tad bit lazy when it comes to reading patterns. This is because online videos are much quicker and easier to follow for some of us. However, this is not ideal, as one should be able to read patterns. By reading through the pattern steps, you'll be able to create a picture in your mind of what the pattern should look like and it will give you a better understanding of what you are doing.

10. Not learning corner-to-corner (C2C) crochet

The C2C method is an important and useful one to learn. You will most definitely use it many times and it is great for making blankets and other garments. Don't avoid this one, try it and practice, you won't be sorry you did.

11. Not learning how to crochet in the round

It is important to see how this works and then try it. This is vital to improving your crochet skills, so don't put off learning how to crochet in the round. It is a valuable technique to know how to use.

12. Not learning how to weave in ends properly

This is one of the most common mistakes made by beginners. It is so easy to just tie knots to the ends, but this is not the proper way of doing it and it is not neat either. Learn to weave the ends into the surface by using the tapestry needle to finish your work off.

13. Worrying about your mistakes

Making mistakes is what helps you to learn and improve your work. Lots of practice and even more patience, as well as some creativity, is what makes a successful crocheter. You will have to undo your stitches from time to time, or even start over again, but that is fine. You are not only learning how to follow instructions; you are also getting used to using your tools and materials so be patient.

14. Trying out complex patterns first

So often, ladies are in a hurry to create the most beautiful colorful garments without being able to master the stitches or change their yarn colors. This could result in a disaster which could also be incredibly discouraging. Just keep it simple until you are confident with basic crochet work.

15. Giving up too soon

It is too easy to just pick up your crochet hook, try out a few stitches, and then give up if they don't work. You might feel as though you are getting nowhere, but that is not true. Give yourself plenty of time to learn the basics because once you can do that, then you can move forward and make so many items. If you cannot get your basic stitches right, then you will have problems making your item. Take it easy and things will slowly start coming together.

Even the most skillful people struggled at first, so go for it and enjoy it!

Chapter 5 Learn the basic steps step by step

If you are a beginner the crochet pattern can certainly look like a foreign language. The first step in learning how to crochet is to learn the basics of crochet. Mastering a very basic crochet needle, there are a few easy-to-learn crochet needles like basketball points, popcorn points, and checkerboard prints! Each point can create a different effect and add interesting and unique textures and patterns to the Afghan crochet. As soon as you understand the crochet needle, it's time to start working on the first novice Afghan crochet pattern! In this e-book, beginners follow one of the Afghan crochet patterns and give themselves a cover, or one to a friend. If you make your first Afghanistan, you will do another, another, another! It is a really addictive hobby. Crochet Afghanistan is a great gift for any occasion, including birthdays, weddings, baby showers, or just because!

Lesson 1: How to Hold the Crochet Hook

Crochet hooks come in many sizes. Very fine steel hooks are used to make intricate doilies and lace. Larger hooks made of aluminum, plastic or wood are used to make afghans, clothing and household items.

The hooks you will use most often are about 6 inches long and are sized alphabetically from B (the smallest) to Q (the largest).

The crochet hook is the most important tool you will use in learning how to crochet, so it is important to understand each part and its function.

When you look at a crochet hook at first glance it looks like a straight piece with a hook on the end. But when you take a closer look, you will see that each hook typically has 5 necessary parts. It is important to know what each part is used for when learning how to crochet.

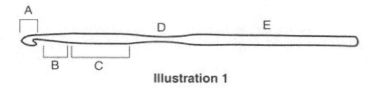

Illustration 1

First is the hook end (A), which is used to hook the yarn and draw it through other loops of yarn (*called stitches*). The throat (B) is a shaped area that helps you slide the stitch up onto the next part of the crochet hook called the working area (C).The finger hold, or thumb rest (D), is the flattened area that helps you grip the hook comfortably, usually with your thumb and third finger. The fifth and final part is the handle (E) which rests under your fourth and fifth fingers and provides balance for easy, smooth work.

It is important that every stitch is made on the working area, never on the throat (B), which would make the stitch too tight, and never on the finger hold (D), which would stretch the stitch.

There are different ways of holding the crochet hook. You will need to experiment and find the way that feels the most comfortable for you. If your hand isn't comfortable, it will cause your hand to cramp up, and your stitches will not be even. We will show you two ways to hold the hook. Again, play around and find the one that feels most natural to you.

The first position is similar to holding a knife, and your hand will grip over the hook. Place your hand over the crochet hook with the handle resting against the palm of your hand and your thumb and third finger gripping the thumb rest.

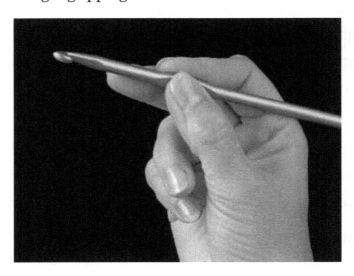

The second position is similar to holding a pencil. Hold the crochet hook as you would a pencil with your thumb and index finger on the finger hold, and the third finger near the tip of the hook.

The crochet hook should be turned slightly toward you, not facing up or down. The crochet hook should be held firmly, but not tightly. At first you will find yourself gripping tightly but over time, once you feel more comfortable, you will find your hand relaxes.

For demonstration purposes, we will be using the pencil hold. Again, find the way that feels most comfortable to you.

Lesson 2: How to Slip Knot and Chain Stitch

Appearance in pattern: ch

Crochet usually begins with a series of chain stitches called a beginning or foundation chain. A slip knot is the first step in most crochet projects.

We will begin by making a slip knot on the crochet hook about 6 inches from the free end of the yarn. You will first start by creating a loop with the yarn. Be sure that the free end of the yarn is dangling behind your loop.

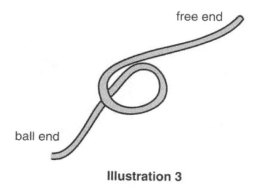

free end

ball end

Illustration 3

Insert the crochet gook through the centre of the loop and hook the free end.

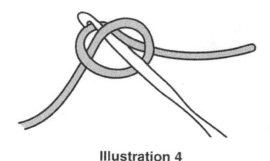

Illustration 4

Pull this through and up onto the working area of the crochet hook.

Illustration 5

Pull the free yarn end to tighten the loop (see illustration 6). The loop on the crochet hook should be firm, but loose enough to slide back and forth easily on the hook. Be sure you still have about a 6-inch yarn end.

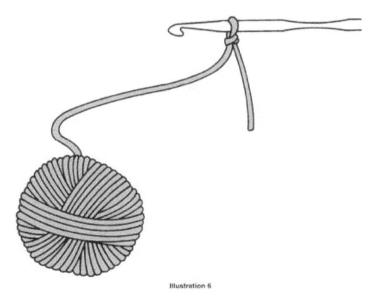

Illustration 6

Once you have the yarn wrapped, hold the base of the slip knot with the thumb and index finger of your left hand.

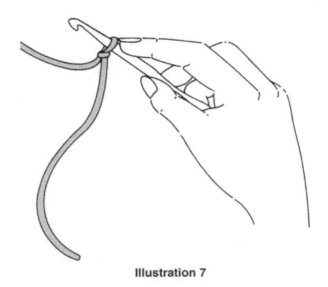

Illustration 7

Bring the yarn over the crochet hook from back to front and hook it.

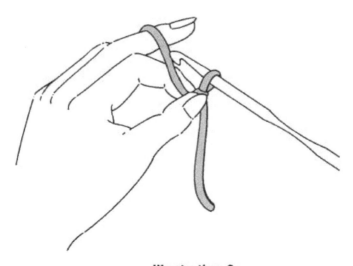

Illustration 8

Draw the hooked yarn through the loop of the slip knot on the hook and up onto the working area of the crochet hook.

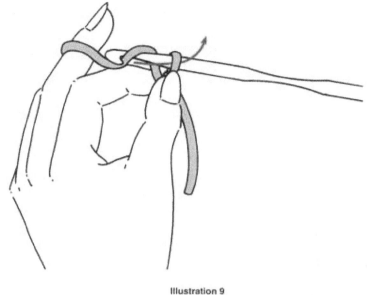

Illustration 9

You have now made one chain stitch.

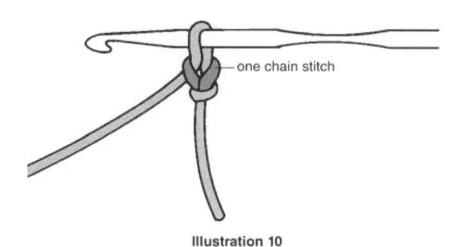

— one chain stitch

Illustration 10

Again, hold the base of the slip knot and bring the yarn over the crochet hook from back to front.

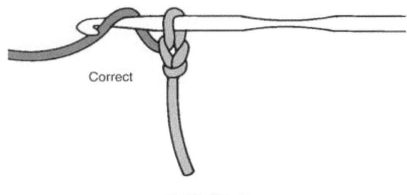

Illustration 11

Hook it and draw though the loop on the hook. You have made another chain stitch. Repeat this step for each additional chain.

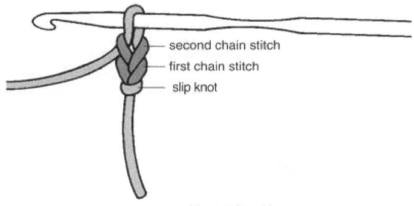

Illustration 12

It is important to note that you should move the left thumb and index finger up the chain close to the crochet hook after each new stitch or two. This helps you control the work. Also, be sure to pull each new stitch up onto the working area of the hook; otherwise your starting chain stiches will become too tight.

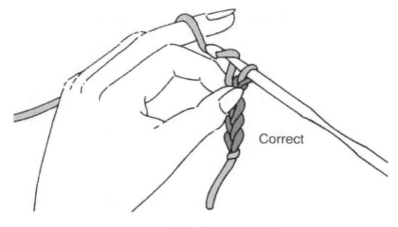

Correct

Illustration 13

Practice making chains until you are comfortable with your grip of the crochet hook and the flow of the yarn. In the beginning, your work will be uneven, with some chain stitches loose and others tight. While you're learning, try to keep the chain stitches loose. As your skill increases, the chain should be firm, but not tight, with all chain stiches even in size.

Lesson 3: How to Single Crochet

Appearance in pattern – sc

Single crochet is the shortest and most basic of all stitches.

Remember, you will never work in the first chain from the crochet hook, unless the pattern you are working specifically directs you to do so.

How to Single Crochet Row 1

Step1: Make a slip knot and chain 6. Skip the first chain from the crochet hook, insert hook in the second chain through the centre of the V and under the back bar of the chain. Bring the yarn over the hook from back to front.

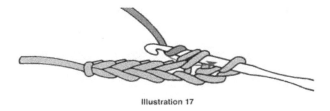

Illustration 17

Draw yarn through chain and up onto the working area of the crochet hook. You now have two loops on the hook.

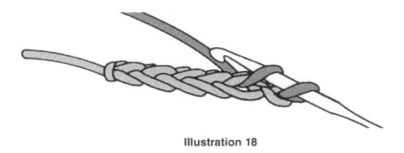

Illustration 18

Step 2: Again, bring the yarn over the hook from back to front, and draw it through both loops on the crochet hook.

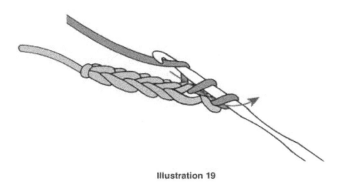

Illustration 19

One loop will remain on the hook. You have made a single crochet.

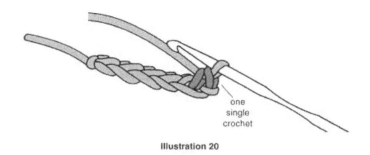

one
single
crochet

Illustration 20

Step 3: Insert hook in the next chain as before, hook the yarn from back to front and draw it through the chain stitch. Yarn over again and draw through both loops. It is important to know that the terms "hook the yarn" and "yarn over" have the same meaning. In both instances, you will bring the yarn over the hook from back to front.

Repeat step 3 in each remaining chain, taking care to work in the last chain, but not in the slip knot. Remember, as you work, to be careful not to twist the chain; keep all the Vs facing you. You have completed one row of single crochet and should now have five stitches in the row.

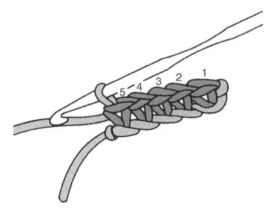

Illustration 21

How to Single Crochet Row 2

To work the second row of single crochet, you need to turn the work counterclockwise, as shown in illustration 22a, so you can work back across the first row. Do not remove the crochet hook as you do this (illustration 22b).

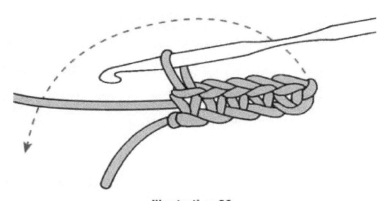

Illustration 22a

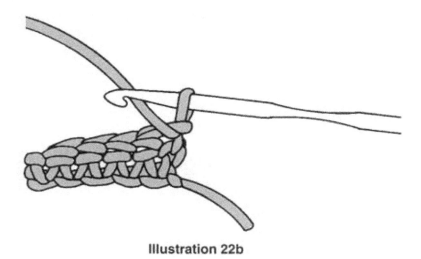

Illustration 22b

This row and all the following rows of single crochet will be worked into a previous row of single crochet, not into the beginning chain as you did before. Remember that when you worked into the starting chain, you inserted the crochet hook through the center of the V and under the bar. This is only done when working into a starting chain.

The first single crochet of the row is worked in the last stitch of the previous row not into the beginning chain.

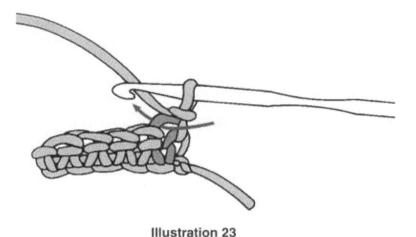

Illustration 23

Insert hook in the last stitch of the previous row under top 2 loops, bring the yarn over the hook from back to front and draw yarn through stitch and up onto the working area of the crochet hook. You now have two loops on the hook. Again, bring the yarn over the hook from back to front and draw it through both loops on the crochet hook.

Work a single crochet into each single crochet to the end, taking care to work in each stitch, especially the last stitch, which is easy to miss.

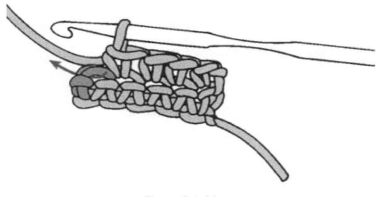

Illustration 24

Let's stop now and count your stitches; you should still have five single crochets on the row. You can continue practicing or fasten off.

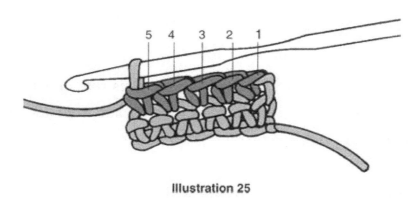

Illustration 25

Fastening off: After the last stitch, cut the yarn, leaving a 6-inch end. As you do when you take your crochet hook out for a break, draw the hook straight up, but this time draw the cut yarn end completely through the stitch. Pull the 6-inch end tight to close.

Lesson 4: How to Half Double Crochet

Appearance in pattern – hdc

This stitch eliminates one step from the double crochet stitch and works up about half as tall. Unless your crochet pattern tells you so, never work in the first chain from the crochet hook.

How to Half Double Crochet in Row 1

Step 1: Start by making a slip knot and chain 13. Bring the yarn once over the crochet hook from back to front, then skip the first two chains before inserting the hook in the third chain from the hook. Take note not to count the loop on the hook as a chain.

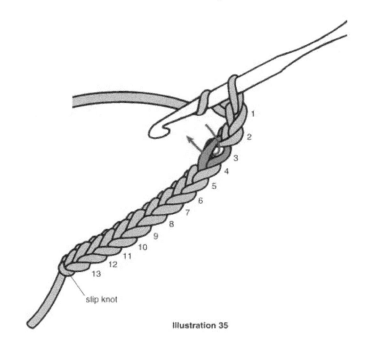

Illustration 35

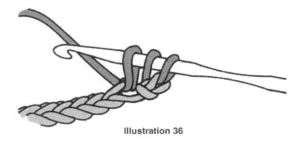

Illustration 36

Step 2: Bring the yarn over the crochet hook and draw it through the chain stitch and up onto the working area of the hook. With this, you will end up with 3 loops on the hook as illustrated below:

Step 3: Bring the yarn over the crochet hook and draw it through all three loops on the hook in one motion.

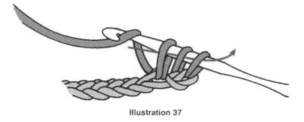

Illustration 37

You will have completed one half double crochet, with one loop remaining on the hook as seen below:

one
half
double
crochet

Illustration 38

To finish the row, continue to work one half double crochet in each remaining chain across the row. Once this row is completed, stop and check the count of your stitches. You should have 12 double half crochets, counting the first two chains you skipped at the beginning of the row as a held double crochet. Then turn our work counterclockwise.

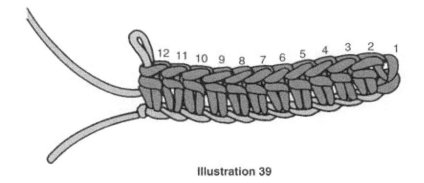

Illustration 39

How to Half Double Crochet in Row 2

Step 1: Start by bringing together the yarn of thread up to the correct height for the next row. To raise the yarn, chain 2 (also called turning chain). Like double crochet, the turning chain counts as a stitch in half double crochet unless your pattern specifies otherwise.

Chain2, skip the first half double of the previous row. Be sure to insert crochet hook under top 2 loops of the stitch, work a half double crochet in the second stitch and in each remaining stitch across the previous row, as below:

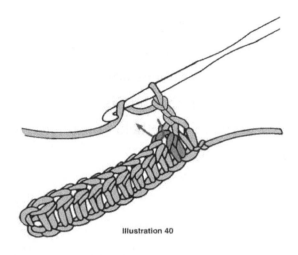

Illustration 40

If not fastening just yet, remember to chain 2 before your first half double crochet.

Fastening off: After the last stitch, cut the yarn. Leave a 6-inch end. Draw the hook straight up, but this time draw the cut yarn end completely through the stitch. Pull the 6-inch end to close.

Lesson 5: How to Treble Crochet

Appearance in pattern – tr (or tr dec if decrease)

This is a tall stitch that works up quickly. Remember to never work in the first chain from the crochet hook, unless the pattern you are working specifically directs you to do so.

How to Treble Crochet in Row 1

Step 1: Begin by making a slip know and chain 15 stitches loosely. Wrap the yarn around the crochet hook from back to front twice, skip the first four chains and then insert the hook into the fifth chain from the hook.

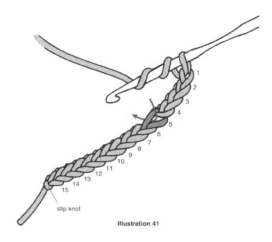

Illustration 41

Step 2: Bring the yarn over the crochet hook from back to front and draw it through the chain stitch and up onto the working area of the hook. You will then have four loops on the hook.

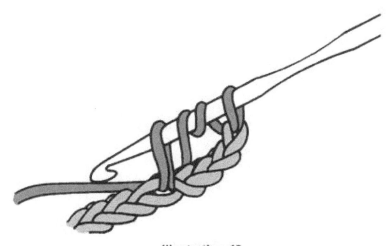

Illustration 42

Step 3: Bring the yarn over the crochet hook and draw it through the first two loops on the hook. You will end up with three loops on the hook as below.

Illustration 43a

Illustration 43b

Step 4: Bring the yarn over the crochet hook again and draw it through the next two loops on the hook. You will end up with two loops remaining on the hook.

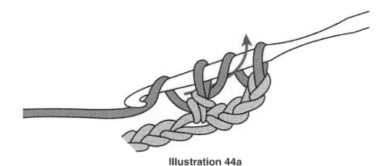

Illustration 44a

Step 5: Bring the yarn over the crochet hook and draw it through both remaining loops on the hook as below.

Illustration 45

You have now completed one treble crochet with one loop still remaining on the hook.

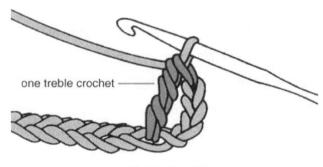

one treble crochet

Illustration 46

Continue working the 5 steps in each of the remaining chains across. When you have worked your last chain, count your stitches. There should be 12 treble crochets, counting the first four chains you previously skipped at the beginning of the row as a treble crochet.

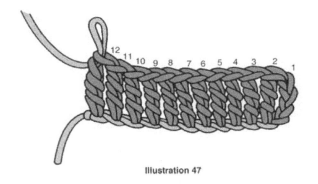

Illustration 47

Turn your work counterclockwise and you can begin working row 2.

How to Treble Crochet in Row 2

To work row 2, you need to bring the yarn or thread up to the correct height for the next row. To raise the yarn, chain four (this is called the turning chain). The four chains in the turning chain just made count as the first treble crochet on the new row. Skip the first stitch and work a treble crochet in the second stitch as in the illustration below. Make sure to insert the crochet hook under top two loops of each stitch.

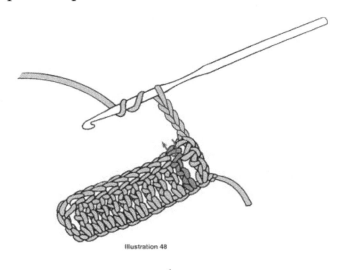

Illustration 48

We will continue to work a treble crochet in each remaining stitch across the previous row. Be sure to work the last treble crochet in the top of the beginning chain form the previous row. Stop and count your treble crochets. There should be 12 stitches. You can keep going or fasten off at this point.

Fastening off – After the last stitch, cut the yarn, leaving a 6-inch end. Like you do when you take your crochet hook out for a break, draw the hook straight up, but this time draw the cut yarn end and completely through the stitch. Pull the 6-inch end to close.

Lesson 6: How to Crochet a Turning chain

At the end of each row of a crochet pattern, it will say "turn" so you are ready to begin working the next row. The proper way is to turn the work around so that the side that was away from you now faces you and the crochet hook is now at the right-hand side of the work, instead of the left. Before starting the next row, you need to remember to raise the crochet hook and working loop up to the same level of the stitch at the beginning of a new row. This is done by working what is called a turning chain. The number of turning chains needed will vary depending on the type of stitch being worked.

Always keep in mind that you should never work into the first chain from the crochet hook unless your instructions state otherwise. Depending on the stitch, you will work into the second, third, fourth, fifth, etc., chain from the hook. Your instructions will always state which chain you will work.

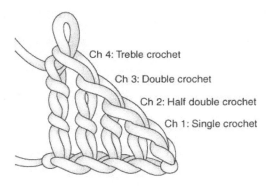

Slip stitch: Work 1 turning chain

Single crochet: Work 1 turning chain

Half double crochet: Work 2 turning chains

Double crochet: Work 3 turning chains

Lesson 7: How to Join Yarn

This lesson will teach you how to join new yarn at the end of a row whenever possible. To do this, work the last stitch with the old yarn until two loops remain on the hook, then with the new yarn complete the stitch.

To join new yarn in the middle of a row, when about 36 inches of the old yarn remains, work several more stitches with the old yarn, working the stitches over the end of new yarn. Then change yarns in previously explained.

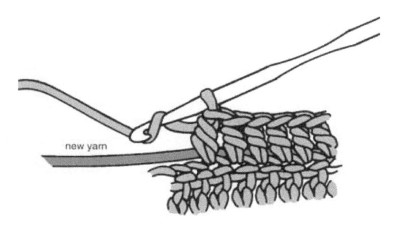

Lesson 8: How to Crochet in the Front and Back loop

Appearance in pattern – front lp or back lp

Working the front or back loops only of a crochet stitch will leave a horizontal bar exposed on the fabric. When working in the back or front loop the crochet fabric becomes more elastic than the traditional way of working under both loops. You can then crochet in the front or back loop only of any crochet stitch.

Below is an example of a traditional crochet stitch wherein you insert the crochet hook from the front of the chain, through the center of the "V" and under the corresponding bar on the back of the same stitch.

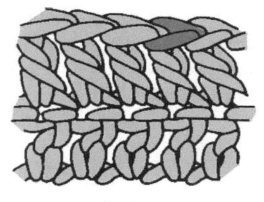

Both Loops

To crochet in the back loop of a stitch, insert your crochet hook underneath the back loop only and make the stitch as indicated in your pattern.

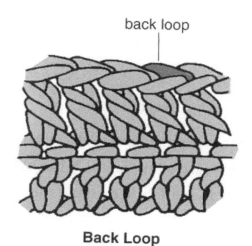

back loop

Back Loop

To crochet in the front loop of a stitch, insert your crochet hook underneath the front loop only and make the stitch as indicated in your pattern.

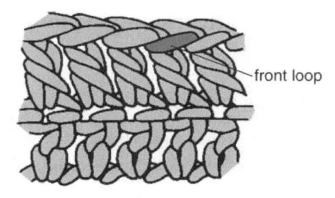

front loop

Front Loop

Lesson 9: Fastening Off

After the last stitch of the last row, cut the yarn, leaving a 6-inch end. Draw the hook straight up and draw the yarn cut end completely through the stitch.

Chapter 6 Patterns and explanations:

Understanding Pattern

Patterns today are written instructions, often wrought with abbreviations. Before, in the early days of crochet, patterns were the actual crocheted item of someone else. For example, a lady wanted to crochet a wrist cuff. A written pattern was not available. Instead, she had to get an actual wrist cuff and painstakingly count the stitches and copy them. Then came the scrapbooks. Fragments of crocheted work were sewn on pieces of paper and bound together like a scrapbook. Some had crocheted samples sewn onto larger fabrics, while some were simply kept in a box or bag. Crochet stitch samples were also made in long and narrow bands.

In 1824, the earliest crochet pattern was printed. The patterns were for making purses from silver and gold threads.

Early crochet books from the 1800s were small. These may be small (4 inches by 6 inches) but they contain a treasure of crochet patterns for lace, cuffs, lace-like collars, insertions, caps (women's, men's and children's), purses and men's slippers. It also contained patterns for white crochet, which were for undergarment trimmings, mats, edgings and insertions. The book recommended materials such as cotton thread, hemp thread, spool yarn and linen thread. Color work was done in chenille, wool and silk yarns, with the occasional silver and gold threads.

The problem about these early patterns was its inaccuracy. For example, the pattern is for an 8-point star, but would turn out to be with only 6 points. These crochet books required the reader to rely more on the woodwork illustrations of as a better guide.

Today, crochet patterns are more systematic, accurate and organized. However, to the uninitiated, looking at a crochet pattern is a lot like looking at letters and numbers with no idea what they meant. Look for the meanings of the abbreviations, which are often printed at the bottom of the pattern. I not, research some of the abbreviations that are unfamiliar.

A crocheter needs to learn the abbreviations and the symbols used in a crochet pattern. Without this knowledge, there will be a very limited number of patterns that a crocheter can work with, as most are written in the crochet language.

Here are a few things to remember when working with patterns:

- Patterns are either made in rounds or rows. The pattern will specify if using either or both.

- Patterns come with a difficulty rating. Crocheters should choose the level best suited to their abilities. That is, beginners should stick to pattern suited for their level while they are still familiarizing themselves with the terms and techniques. Move to higher difficulty levels after gaining enough experience and mastery of the required crochet skills.

- Always count the stitches made while working then after reaching the end of the row or round.

- Always check the gauge, especially if the project has to turn out the exact size and shape as indicated in the pattern.

- Learning to read crochet patterns require practice and experience. Be patient and don't get this sc outraged.

How To Read A Crochet Pattern?

Crochet patterns would often only list the abbreviations and the number of stitches required for each row or round. Some patterns would also use abbreviations for other instructions such as when to turn or when to begin and end.

The simplest crochet pattern would look like this:

Row 1: Use a size E crochet hook, ch15, single crochet 2nd ch from hook and for each ch, turn.

(14 single crochet)

This can look more like a foreign language to the uninitiated. This is still the simplest of crochet patterns. Translated, the line means:

Row 1: With a crochet hook size E, make 15 chain stitches. Starting on the 2nd stitch from the hook, make a single crochet stitch across the chain stitches. Then make a turning stitch. by the end of the row, there should be 12 single crochet stitches done.

Circle Patterns

Circles are also common in crochet. it starts with a center ring, which is the foundation of all rounds, as foundation chain is to working in rows. The center ring is created either by making a ring from chain stitches or from in single chain stitch. The first method creates a hole in the middle of the circle crochet work. The second method has an inconspicuous middle.

Working With A Hole As A Center Ring

This is the most common way of making a center ring. A row of chain stitches is created then looped off to make a ring. The hole in the middle is determined by how many chain stitches were made at the beginning. It also determines how many stitches can be made through the center ring. Avoid making the chain stitch too long because the resulting ring would be too large and unsteady.

1.   Ch6 (make 6 chain stitches).

2.   Place the crochet hook into the 1st chain stitch, the one farthest from the crochet hook and next to the slip knot. This will now form a ring.

3. Do 1 yarn over.

4. Through the chain stitch and through the loop resting on the crochet hook, pull the yarn. This completes the center ring with a hole visible in the middle.

Working with a hole for a center is easy because the stitches are made by going through the center hole instead of into the actual chain stitches of the ring.

1. From the finished center ring above, make ch1 as a turning chain to be used for the single crochet of the first row.

2. Place the crochet hook through the center ring.

3. Make 1 yo. Pull the wrapped yarn all the way through the hole (center ring).

4. Make another yo and pull it through the 2 loops resting in the crochet hook. This finishes 1 single crochet (single crochet).

5. Continue making single crochet through the center hole until it can't fit anymore.

Working Into The Chain Stitch

This is another way of working in rounds. This is used when the pattern calls for a very small or barely noticeable center hole. Generally, one starts with a slipknot and ch1, then add the number of chain stitches required for a turning chain. For example, make 1 chain stitch then another 3 if using double crochet because the turning chains for dc is 3 chain stitches.

1. Ch1.

2.	If using dc, make ch3.

3.	Perform 1 yarn over and place the hook into the center of the 4th chain stitch from the hook. This is the 1st ch made and is located next to the slipknot.

4.	Make 1 double crochet into this chain stitch. continue making dc on the other chain stitches.

To the uninitiated, a crochet pattern might look like it's written in a completely different language, and in a way, it is. Designers and crocheters use a language of abbreviations and conventions that are standardized, which makes it easy for anyone who understands this language to follow a pattern. The following is a breakdown of the most common ways information is relayed in a crochet pattern – and what it all means.

Materials

The materials is where the designer indicates everything the crocheter will need to complete the pattern. This usually includes the yarn, hook size, and any extra notions or items. Sometimes patterns include the brand names of yarn or other items, but sometimes they merely contain the type of item needed (Lion Brand Fishermen's Wool Yarn versus 100 percent worsted weight yarn, for example). One important item to pay attention to in the materials is the amount of yarn needed; little is more frustrating that running out of yarn in the middle of a project!

Gauge

Gauge is a dreaded word to even experienced crocheters, but it doesn't have to be. Put simply, gauge is the measurement of the number of crochet stitches and rows per inch of fabric. Why is this important? Because achieving the proper gauge ensures that the finished item will turn out the correct size. Ignore gauge, and what's supposed to be a cropped, snug cardigan might become a housedress.

A pattern will indicate gauge either over 1 inch or 4 inches of stitches. For example, a gauge might read: '3 stitches and 4 rows over 1 inch in single crochet.' This means that if the crocheter works a fabric in single crochet, he or she should have 3 stitches and 4 rows in every inch when using the hook size indicated in the materials.

Before beginning a project, the crocheter checks that they are getting gauge by crocheting at least a 4-inch by 4-inch swatch in the pattern stitch (in the example, single crochet), then blocking it, then measuring it carefully. If the gauge matches that given, it's okay to start the project. If the gauge does not match, the crocheter needs to change either the hook size or the yarn until they get gauge. This is necessary because small differences in gauge can equal big differences in a finished item: a row of 30 single crochet at 3 stitches per inch will be 10 inches long, whereas a row of 30 single crochet at 4 stitches per inch will only be 7.5 inches long – not an unimportant difference.

The crocheter should generally change the hook size before changing the yarn. If the gauge is smaller than that given (e.g., 2 stitches per inch instead of 3), the hook is too large. If the gauge is larger than that given (e.g., 4 stitches per inch instead of 3), the hook is too small. Row gauge is much more adaptable in crochet, but the crocheter should still aim to get the gauge of both.

Note that with some projects, gauge is more important than with others. For items with a lot of shaping, including sweaters, mittens, socks, and hats, gauge is critical. For items that are more 'one size fits all', a small difference in gauge might be okay – a scarf that is an inch wider than the designer intended isn't necessarily the end of the world.

Abbreviations

The abbreviations includes all of the abbreviations used in the pattern. Many times, this includes instructions for working special stitches. If a crocheter doesn't understand some of the stitches used in the pattern, the abbreviations is a good place to look for help. Many abbreviations are standardized, so as crocheters gain practice reading patterns, they learn to immediately recognize single crochet for single crochet, dc for double crochet, and so on.

Instructions

The instructions are the meat of the pattern, the place where the designer tells the crocheter what to do to make the item. For the most part, designers are explicit – 'Chain 3, work 3 for turning chain, double crochet into third chain from hook' – but a few common shortcuts are used as well, including:

Asterisks – Asterisks are used to indicate repeats of of patterns. A pattern might read: 'Chain 1, slip stitch into second chain from hook, *3 single crochet, ch 2, 3 single crochet*, repeat from * to * three times, chain 1, turn'. The stitches within the asterisks are repeated three times in the sequence they're given *after* the first time they're worked. So, in total, the asterisk would be repeated four times.

Parentheses – Parentheses are used to indicate repeats, often within asterisks. Changing the example, the crocheter might see: '...*3 single crochet, (ch 2, single crochet) twice, 3single crochet*, repeat from * to * three times.' To work the directions inside the asterisks, the crocheter would work 3 single crochet, 2 chains, 1 single crochet, 2 chains, 1 single crochet, then 3 more single crochet. Then the crocheter would repeat the instructions inside the asterisks the number of times called for.

Many crochet patterns are also broken down into rows (for flat crochet) and rounds (for circular crochet). Pattern repeats are often made up of a number of rows or rounds, which the designer will indicate in the pattern. At the end of the pattern, the designer will include any special finishing instructions, such as how to add embellishments or borders.

New crocheters should remember that although these are common conventions used in pattern writing, there are exceptions; designers are individuals, and some have their own unique way of writing instructions.

Chapter 7 For Beginners

How To Read Stitch Patterns

You'll find stitch patterns written in two different ways. The first is the most typical, and will be found in vintage patterns, as well as many modern American and British patterns. This is a fully written out stitch pattern, using typical and traditional stitch notation. Below, you'll find a list of common abbreviations, and a few notes about translation issues, as well as a sample pattern and a breakdown of what it means. Some modern designers in the west, as well as Japanese crochet patterns do not rely upon written out notation, but on a graphic representation of crochet stitches. These look nothing at all like craft charts you might have used, like those for cross stitching or knitting. They are, in fact, rather pictorial, with picture symbols written out for each round or row. Once you're used to reading crochet charts, you'll find you can do so with relative ease.

- -Charts are much more commonly used for doilies or shawls, rather than simple projects, like a hat or afghan.

- -Charts are rarely used for repeated stitch patterns, but can be.

Written crochet patterns are still the most common in America and Britain. They are relatively easy to use, and pattern notation is largely standardized.

approx	approximately
beg	beginning
blo	back loop only
cc	contrast color
ch	chain
cl	cluster
cont	continue
dc	double crochet
dec	decrease
ea	each
gm	grams
gr	group
hdc	half double crochet
hk	hook
inc	increase
incl	including
lp	loop

mc	main color
pat	pattern
rem	remaining
rep	repeat
rnd(s)	round(s)
RS	right side
sc	single crochet
sl	slip
slst	slip stitch
sk	skip
sp	space
st(s)	stitch(es)
tog	together
tr / tc	triple (treble) crochet
WS	wrong side
yo	yarn over

Which of these are the most common? For crocheters, they're fairly simple: yo, ch, sc, hdc, dc, tc. Nearly all crochet patterns are made up of these basic stitches, put together in different ways. Most patterns also include a key explaining specific abbreviations. You may find this especially helpful if the pattern includes particular stitch patterns or combinations or if you've not crocheted for some time.

Let's look at a simple shell stitch pattern. This pattern can be used for a variety of different projects, making a pretty and feminine garment or blanket. It's relatively quick to work, and easily memorized.

- Make a chain of any length desired, plus 3 stitches for turning.

- Row 1: Make 5 DC in the 3rd st from end, * skip 2 ch, make 1 SC in next stitch, skip 2 and make 5 DC in next stitch *.

- Row 2. Ch. 3, and turn. Work 4 DC into SC * 1 SC into 3rd DC of previ-ous row, 5 DC into SC of previous row. Repeat from * across row.

- Repeat Row 2 to desired length.

- Let's take a longer look at this in a written out form:

- -Row 1: Make 5 double crochet stitches in the third stitch from the end of the chain. *Skip 2 chains, make one single crochet in the next stitch, skip 2 chains and make 5 double crochet stitches in the next stitch.*

- Row 2: Chain 3 and turn. Work 4 double crochet into single crochet. Work one single crochet into 3rd double crochet of the previous row, 5 double crochet into the single crochet of the previous row. Repeat from * to end.

- With just a little practice, the abbreviations will become second nature. You'll find them used throughout the patterns in this book.

- Do note: If you're an American and using a British pattern or you're British and using an American pattern, there's a bit of a quirk between the two languages.

British Notation	American Notation
double crochet (dc)	single crochet (sc)
half treble (htr)	half double crochet (hdc)
treble (tr)	double crochet (dc)
double treble (dtr)	treble (tr)
triple treble (trtr)	double treble (dtr)
miss	skip
tension	gauge
yarn over hook (yoh)	yarn over (yo)

Do you see the difference? The UK doesn't use the term single crochet; a single crochet is called a double, and a double crochet is called a treble. The treble crochet is called a double treble. Reviewing the pattern key can help you to know whether you're working with a British or American pattern, but it's an easy adjustment, especially as you get used to working the pattern.

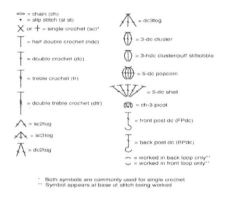

The key above illustrates crochet chart symbols. The symbols themselves are universal, but do notice that the language refers to American crochet notation and work the stitches accordingly. When assembled to form a chart, the symbols might look like

You may notice something about this chart right away. It creates a visual very similar to the finished work, making it easy to realize what your project should look like, even if you don't have a picture of the finished work.

- Round 1: Ch 16, join with a sl st.

- Round 2: Ch 3, work one dc in first chain of previous rnd. *work one dc in next stitch, 2 dc in next around* join with a sl st. (24)

- Round 3: Ch 3, sk 1 dc, sc in next, *ch 3, sk 1 dc, sc in next* join with a sl st.

- Round 4: Ch 3, *1 dc in first sc, sk 1 ch, *10 dc in 2nd ch stitch, sk 1 ch, 1 sc in sc* to last ch 3 loop. 9 dc in 2nd ch st, sl st to join to 3rd ch in initial ch 3.

- Round 5: Sc in 6th dc of last dc cluster, ch 5, dc in sc of prev round, ch5, *sc in 6th dc of cluster, ch10, dc in sc of prev round, ch 5, dc in sc of prev round, ch5* join with sl st

- Round 6: Working backwards to reverse direction, slip stitch in the first 5 ch stitches to the left of your hook. This returns you to the corner of your work. Ch 8, sc in third ch of ch 5 of previous round. *Ch 5 sc in third ch of ch 5 of previous round. Ch5, dc 3 in 6th ch of ch 10 of prev round, ch 3, dc3 in same space*. On last repeat, dc 2, using first 3 chains of initial chain 8 to make the third dc. Join with sl st at third chain.

- Round 7: Working backwards again, sl st in first 5 stitches to reach the corner of your work. Ch 8, sc in third ch of ch 5 of previous round. *Ch 5 sc in third ch of ch 5 of previous round. Ch5, sc in third ch of ch 5 of prev round, dc 3 in 6th ch of ch 10 of prev round, ch 3, dc3 in same space*. On last repeat, dc 2, using first 3 chains of initial chain 8 to make the third dc. Join with sl st at third chain.

- Round 8: Working backwards again, sl st in first 5 stitches to reach the corner of your work. Ch 8, sc in third ch of ch 5 of previous round. *Ch 5 sc in third ch of ch 5 of previous round. Ch5, sc in third ch of ch 5 of prev round, Ch5, sc in third ch of ch 5 of prev round, dc 3 in 6th ch of ch 10 of prev round, ch 3, dc3 in same space*. On last repeat, dc 2, using first 3 chains of initial chain 8 to make the third dc. Join with sl st at third chain.

- (Note: Rounds 6, 7 and 8 are nearly identical, with the addition of one more ch5 loop per side in each round)

As you can see, that's a very cumbersome pattern written out. It's much easier to follow and understand working from a pictorial chart. This is the benefit of charts for complex and lacy work. If you'd like, you can even make your own charts, either by hand or using online charting software.

Lightweight Textured Stitch Patterns

1. Textured Single Crochet

- Foundation chain: multiple of 2 + 3 stitches

- Row 1: Work 1 sc in 3rd ch from hook, *sk 1 ch, 2 sc into next ch, rep from * to last 2 ch, sk 1 ch, 1 sc into last ch, turn.

-Row 2: Ch1 (counts as first sc), 1 sc in first sc, *sk 1 sc, 2 sc into next sc, rep from * to last 2 sts to last 2 sts, sk 1 sc, 1 sc in top of the chain used to turn.

-Repeat row 2 to desired length.

2. Crochet Seed Stitch

- Foundation chain: multiple of 2 + 1

- Row 1: Sc in the second chain from hook, dc in next. Repeat to end of row.

- Row 2: Ch 1, sc in first stitch, dc in next. Repeat to end of row.

- Repeat row 2 to desired length.

3. Ribbed Seed Stitch

Working through the back loop creates the ribbed texture.

- Foundation chain: multiple of 2 + 1

- Row 1: Sc in the back loop in 2nd ch from hook, dc in the back loop in next. Repeat to end of row.

- Row 2: Ch 1, sctbl in first stitch, dctbl in next. Repeat to end of row.

- Repeat row 2 to desired length.

4. Waffle Stitch

- Foundation row: Multiple of 4 plus 3 stitches

- Row 1: Work one row in single crochet. Ch3, turn.

- Row 2: Dc in next, *ch2, sk 2 sts, dc in next 2 sts. Rep from * across. Ch3, turn.

- Row 3: Dc in next dc. *1 tr in each of the next 2 sk sts, working each treble behind the ch2 of the previous row. Dc in next 2. Repeat from * across. Ch3, turn.

- Rep rows 2 & 3 to desired length.

5. Waffle Stitch Variation

This stitch works particularly well in hand dyed or variegated yarns.

- Row 1: Ch 23. Sc in the second ch from hook and in each chain stitch across. Ch3, turn.

- Row 2: Dc in next, *ch2, sk next 2 sts dc in next 2. Rep from * across. End with a dc in last 2 sts. Ch3, turn.

- Row 3: Dc in next st, *Tr in first sk st working in front of ch2 sp. Tr in the next skipped stitch, inserting the hook behind the ch 2 space. Dc in next 2 dc. Rep from * across. Ch3, turn.

- Repeat row 2 and 3 as desired.

- Finish with a row beginning with ch1, sc across.

6. Brick Stitch

- Foundation Chain: Multiple of 4

- Row 1: Work 3 dc in the 4th chain from the hook, * sk 3 chains, sc in next chain, chain 3, 3 dc in same chain. Repeat from * across row, ending with sc.

- Row 2: Work 3 chains to turn. 3 dc in sc of prev. row. * sc in next ch3 space of prev row, chain 3, 3 dc in same ch3 space. Repeat from * across row. End with sc in last ch3 of prev row.

- Repeat row 2 to length needed.

7. Shell Stitch

You can vary shell stitch by replacing the double crochet stitches with either half double or treble crochet stitches; you may also work more or fewer stitches in each shell-shape. You may also skip more stitches between shells for a slightly different appearance. The shell stitch is slightly lacy, producing a relatively feminine appearance.

- Foundation Chain: Multiple of 6 stitches plus 1

- Row 1: Ch 1, 1 sc in 2nd chain from the hook, * skip 2 chains, 5 dc in next chain, skip 2 chain, 1 sc in next ch , rep from * to end of row. Turn.

- Row 2: Ch 3 (counts as first dc), 2 dc in same st as ch3 just made, * skip 2 dc, 1 sc in next dc (center st of the 5dc shell), skip 2 dc, 5 dc in next sc **, repeat * to ** to end of row, ending the last repeat with 3 dc in last sc, skip turning chain. Turn.

- Row 3: Ch 1, 1 sc in first st, * sk 2 dc, 5 dc in next sc, sk 2 dc, 1 sc in next dc , repeat from * to end of row, to end with sc.

- Repeat rows 2 and 3 to length desired.

8. Wave Stitch

This stitch works best worked in three different colors, but can be done in a single color if you prefer.

- Foundation chain: Multiple of 14

- Row 1: In 3rd chain from hook, dc 3.*Sk 3 chains, sc in next 7 ch. Sk 3 ch, 7 dc in next ch. *

- Row 2: Ch 1, sc across row

- Row 3: Ch1, sc in next 4 stitches, *Sk 3 ch, 7 dc in next stitch. Sk 3, 7 sc to last Sk 3, then work 4 sc.

- Row 4: Repeat row 2

- Repeat rows 1-4 to desired length.

Chapter 8 For Advanced

Pineapple Lace

This is different from the fruit which it is named after and its made up of the simplest stitches though it looks so fancy.

Bullion Stitch

Go with the bullion stitch if you want a stitch whose texture is heavy. Pulling the hook through them all at one and working which quite big amounts of yarn overs, you will get lots of yarn bursts which are almost like 3D.

Loop Stitch

We expect the loop stitch to get its shinning moment since tassels are having a moment, It's a fur on adorable amigurumi projects and great at embellishing accessories and pillows.

Crocodile Stitch

This crocodile stitch know how to make a splach though its so new to the world of crochet. And to give more stability to everything, you work the scales over a background of mesh. It can be useful in making jewelry, edgings and pillows.

Starting and finishing project

Starting project

Before making any stitches, it's important to understand how to hold a crochet hook. Part of this is determined by handedness; left-handed individuals don't have to learn to crochet in the typical manner (i.e., holding the hook in the right hand), but they should keep in mind that most patterns are written for right-handed crocheters. This may make it worthwhile to learn to crochet with the right hand, but directions can be reversed with practice, so left-handers are under no duress to use their non-dominant hand. Because the majority of individuals are right-handed, this work focuses on learning to crochet with the right hand.

Ways to hold a crochet hook are numerous, but the two most common are referred to as the knife hold and the pencil hold. Neither is better than the other, only different. New crocheters are encouraged to try both holds to find the one that is the most comfortable for them.

With the knife hold, the hand faces downward with the hook under the palm, much the way one would hold a knife. The pencil hold is the opposite: The palm faces upward with the hook grasped between the thumb and two forefingers, like holding a pencil.

Finishing project.

Properly finishing a crocheted piece is important for several reasons. First, the finishing process will settle the stitches, giving the piece a professional look. Second, finishing allows the crocheter to form the piece into the correct shape and straighten any shaping issues. Third, finishing items properly makes seaming and adding embellishments easier. Any way you look at it, then, finishing is a necessary part of the crocheting process.

The two main steps in finishing are weaving in the yarn ends and blocking. While many crafters don't see either process as particularly 'fun', learning to perform them properly does take some of the anxiety out of the work. Hopefully, after finishing a few projects, blocking and weaving in ends will start to feel like just one more step in a crochet project.

Weaving in ends

Every piece will have a yarn tail at the beginning and end of the work. Those crochet projects that have multiple yarn joins or colors will have more. For projects with many yarn tails, yarn ends should be woven in during the crocheting if at all possible, simply because leaving them all to the end can make the weaving process seem like a herculean task. The crocheter should also always leave at least a 6-inch tail of yarn; any shorter, and it may be too difficult to 'hide' the yarn inside the work.

In crocheting, there are two popular methods of weaving in ends: crocheting over them and weaving them in with a yarn needle. Both ways give desirable results, so it's up to crocheters to decide which method they prefer. New crocheters should remember, however, that if their favorite method isn't working for a project, it's okay to try the other way.

Crocheting over yarn ends is performed exactly as it sounds: The crocheter places the yarn tail along the row of crochet stitches being worked and crochets over it with the stitches. Many crocheters prefer this method simply because it doesn't leave the yarn tails to the end of the project. Of course, crocheting over yarn ends can also be tricky – circular motifs with many open areas, for example, might not lend themselves to this method. In these cases, it's also possible to crochet the yarn tail into the piece; the tail is held along with the working yarn and the crocheter works as normal until the tail is used up.

Above: Crocheting over yarn ends

Weaving in ends with a yarn needle can take longer, but it is a useful method to know for hiding ends in 'tricky' areas. The goal is to secure the end as much as possible while ensuring that it can't be seen. The end should always be woven into the wrong side of the work; for works that have no 'wrong' side (such as scarves), the crocheter will have to choose a side.

To weave in the end with a yarn needle, the crocheter can run the yarn under a line of stitches for about an inch or so. Then, instead of snipping the yarn, the crocheter runs the tail back under half of the stitches. Before snipping the yarn, it's also helpful to pull the end taut so that it springs into position under the stitches.

Chapter 9 Patterns and Explanations for Children

Wrist Warmers

We'll start with something every kid needs at some point; wrist warmers. These wrist warmers should end up being about six and a half inches long and two inches tall.

The materials you're going to need for this pattern are three different colors of medium weight yarn, a 5.5mm Tunisian crochet hook, a yarn needle, and a pair of scissors.

The gauge isn't very important with this pattern but to give you an idea 7 rows should be about 2 inches thick. The pattern makes two of the warmers, or enough for one kid, and is laid out below.

Row 1: Start by chaining ten with your first color. If you chain ten and it doesn't look tall enough you can chain a few more. Just remember to chain the same amount further down the line. Change to the second color in the last chain and simple stitch starting from the second chain from the hook, then in each chain across. Change to the third color at the beginning of the reverse pass, then change back to the first color in the last simple stitch of the reverse pass.

Row 2: Simple stitch in the second stitch from the hook and in each stitch across. Switch to your second color at the start of the reverse pass. Then switch to your third color at the last simple stitch of the reverse pass.

Row 3: Simple stitch in the second stitch from the hook and in each stitch across. Switch to your first color at the start of the reverse pass. Then switch to your second color at the last simple stitch of the reverse pass.

Row 4: Simple stitch in the second stitch from the hook and in each stitch across. Switch to your third color at the start of the reverse pass. Then switch to your first color at the last simple stitch of the reverse pass.

After that you need to repeat rows 2-4 seven more times at the least. Or just keep going until the wrist warmer is large enough for you. Then move on to row five.

Row 5: Slip stitch in the second stitch from the hook and in each stitch across. All you have to do after that is just finish off.

To make your button you need to use this pattern:

Round 1: Chain two then five sc in the second chain from the hook.

Round 2: Use 4 sc in the same chain, overlapping your previous round. Then finish off.

The strap is pretty easy. To do that you just have to chain six and then finish off.

To finish off the wrist warmers properly sew a button to one end of the wrist warmer and then sew the strap to the opposite end.

Baby Blanket

Use baby soft yarn, blue for a boy and pink for a girl.

The point of this pattern is for you to get used to the different texture of the different yarns, and learn how to work with different kinds of fibers.

Cast on 50, then Tunisian crochet across the row. Chain 1, turn, and single crochet back across the other side. Repeat this until you are happy with the length of the blanket.

Tie off securely, babies are wiggly and you don't want them to get their fingers stuck in any loose threads!

Perfect Pillows

2 skeins of acrylic yarn in the color of your choice.

Cast on 25. Single crochet across the row, then chain 1 and turn. Repeat this until you have a square, and tie off. Make another square patch the same size as the first, and tie off.

Next, using a yarn needle, sew the two squares together, leaving a little side open for the stuffing. Turn the right way, stuff the pillows until they are plump, and sew the opening shut. Add a nice fringe border to make them look flirty.

Miniature Hat Ornament

This great little hat is the ideal decoration for a Christmas tree, or just a wonderful little project for you to have a go at. The finished size of the hat is about 1 and three quarter inches across and high.

You're going to need nine yards of worsted weight yarn, an I hook (that's 5.5mm) and a yarn needle. The gauge should be about four stitches for an inch but gauge isn't overly important here.

Here's the pattern:

Row 1: Chain sixteen and then skip the first chain. Pull up the loop through the back bump of each stitch so you have sixteen loops on your hook. Then yarn over and pull through one loop. Yarn over then pull through two loops and repeat that until only one loop is left.

Rows 2-8: Skip the first vertical bar. Insert the hook from the front to the back between strands of the next vertical bar. Yarn over and then pull up a loop. Repeat that across. To return you yarn over and pull through one loop. Then yarn over and pull through two loops until one loop is left.

Row 9: Skip the first vertical bar then insert the hook from the front to the back between strands of the next vertical bar. You yarn over, and pull up a loop, then repeat that across. To return just yarn over and pull the loop through all the other loops in the row, going one or two at a time. That's how you gather the crown of the hat. Finish off and then pull tight.

To finish you turn so the wrong side is facing and whipstitch the vertical edge closed. If you've done it right the bottom edge should flip up naturally. Secure the yarn to the inside of the crown and turn the right side out, and make a loop about three inches high. Knot the yarn near the crown, secure the yarn inside of the hat, and weave in all the ends. There you have it; one tiny little hat.

Tunisian Scarf

One common item that's made with crocheting is a scarf. Here's a look at just one of the many kinds of scarves you can make with Tunisian crocheting. Or, indeed, any kind of crocheting.

You're going to need 7 skeins of wool and a size J (6 mm) Afghan crochet hook. Remember Afghan crochet is just another way of saying Tunisian crochet. The gauge is that 14 stitches comes to about 4 inches.

To get started you need to work your foundation chain. For this pattern you need to chain 42 stitches. When you've made your foundation it's time to work with row 1.

Forward Row 1: Insert your hook through the space between the vertical strands, then yarn over and pull a loop through the hook. Insert the hook into the next space, yarn over, and pull the loop through onto the hook. Repeat that until you get to the last space, which needs to be skipped. Instead you insert your Afghan hook into the chain stitch at the edge. Pull the loop through onto the hook.

Return row 1: Chain one stitch, yarn over, and pull the loop through the next two stitches on the hook. Repeat until you get to the end, ending with one loop on the hook.

Forward row 2: Insert the hook into the second space, yarn over, and pull the loop through onto the hook. Insert the hook into the third space, yarn over, and pull the loop through onto the hook. Repeat that to the end of the row, including the last space. Insert your Afghan hook into the chain stitch at the edge, pull the loop through onto the hook.

Return row 2: Just do the same thing you did for the first return row. Then you just repeat these steps until the scarf is as long as you want it. The original pattern calls for 70 inches but that's way too long for a kid.

Now it's time for the finish.

This time when you do the first forward row insert the hook into the first space, yarn over, and pull through two loops on the hook. Repeat this until the end when you should have one loop left on the hook. Then you cut the yarn and pull through the remaining loop.

With the right side facing you, as you should for Tunisian crochet, join the yarn and make a single crochet into each stitch along the edge you're going to bind off. Cut the yarn and pull through the remaining loop. Repeat that for the cast-on edge and then weave in all the ends and block how you want to finish completely.

Faux Knit Headband

This headband is great for keeping your kids heads warm and it's as soft as it looks.

You need two colorways of worsted weight yarn, a size J Tunisian crochet hook, and a yarn needle. Safety pins will help but aren't necessary. There isn't much of a gauge in this pattern either. Just keep going until it's the right size. You want to make one that's a few inches short because the yarn does stretch.

To begin with make a foundation chain nine stitches long using your first color.

Row 1: Work your forward pass in the first color. Drop the first color at the end and work your way back using the second color.

Row 2: Work the forward pass in the second color. Drop the second color at the end and work your way back using the first color.

Just repeat that until the headband is as long as you need it to be. When you finish the last row use a slip stitch in each stitch across.

When the headband is the right size it's time to finish it up. Cut the yarn, but leave a long trail of about ten inches long. Thread your yarn needle (you can also use a tapestry needle for this step) and stitch the two ends together. Weave in the ends and turn the headband right side out and you're good to go.

Row 4: Skip first vertical bar. Working as for a Tunisian full stitch, insert the hook under the first horizontal bar and pull up a loop. Still working as for a Tunisian full stitch, insert hook under the next 16 horizontal bars, pulling up loops for each. Close the same as before.

Row 5: Skip first horizontal and vertical bars. Working as for Tunisian full stitch, insert hook under the remaining horizontal bars, even the ones from row 2-4. Pull up loops in each one too. Working as for Tunisian knot stitch, pull up a loop in the last vertical bar, giving you 38 loops on the hook. Close by yarning over and pull through one loop on the hook 7 times. Yarn over and pull through 3 loops on the hook 8 times. Yarn over and pull through 3 loops on hook. Yarn over and pull through two loops repeatedly until done.

Bind off by skipping the first vertical bar. Then, working for TFS, slip under each horizontal bar across. Then cut off the remaining yarn. With the yarn needle and about 18 inches of yarn seam the last row to the foundation row. Weave the yarn loosely along the edges of each row at the top of your hat using a different piece of yarn. Cinch gently to draw the hole together and sew it together to maintain the closure. Weave all the ends in securely and flip the hat "inside out" to finish.

Tunisian Crochet Cellphone Bag

Do your children have cell phones? If they do you can use this design to create a handy little bag for them to keep it in.

You need some size ten cotton thread in green and greensh grey. Or just two colors that fit well together. A 3.5 mm steel crochet hook. A sea shell bead, and some Velcro fastening finish the list.

To make the body use a double strand of green to chain 18 + 2. Use a basic Tunisian stitch on these 18 chains for 44 rows. Then fasten up.

The flap is a little more complicated. Join a double strand of greenish grey at the beginning of the last row and work on sc in each stitch across. Then turn.

Row 2: chain three, dec over next two sc, 1 sc in each sc across to the last sc. Then dec over the last two and turn.

Row 3: Chain 2, 1 sc in each sc across to the end. Turn.

Then you repeat row 2 and 3 until 2 sc remain. Pass the thread through both and fasten off.

For the strap you knit an I-cord using one strand of green and one strand of grey. You do this by using a pair of double pointed 3mm needles, cast on 3 stitches. Knit across. Slide the stitches across the needle to the right edge and, bringing the thread to the right and behind the work, knit across again. Keep that up until the strap is as long as it needs to be and cast off the three stitches together to finish.

Finish the bag properly by sewing the sides together by using a weave stitch. Use the grey to crochet a row of sc along the margins of the flap. Attach the seashell bead to the top of the flap. Then sew the I-cord and Velcro fastening in place.

Tunisian Stitch Neck Warmer

This great little neck warmer is idea for keeping your loved ones necks warm in the cold weather.

You need two colors of medium weight yarn, a size I crochet hook, a yarn needle, and a pair of scissors. The gauge is that 7 rows should equal 2 inches.

Use the green yarn to chain 20, or as wide as you'd like the neck warmer to be.

Row 1: Work a simple stitch in the second chain from the hook, and in each chain across.

Row 2-53: Work the simple stitch in the second stitch and in each stitch across

Row 54: Work a simple stitch in the second stitch and in each stitch across. This time change to brown yarn in the last simple stitch.

Row 55-74: Work a simple stitch in the second stitch and then each stitch across.

Row 75: Work a slip stitch in the second stitch and then in each stitch across. Finish off.

To make the button (and you need to make two) just follow this pattern.

Row 1: Use the green yarn to chain 4, slip stitch in the forth chain from the hook to form a loop.

Row 2: Work ten sc in the loop.

Row 3: Work ten sc in the loop, overlapping the previous row.

Row 4: Work eight sc in the loop, overlapping the previous one again, and finish off.

To make the button strap, and again you need to make 2, use this pattern.

Row 1: Chain 15, then slip stitch in the first chain to form a loop, then finish off.

Use a yarn needle to sew the buttons onto the brown end of the neck warmer, and the button straps onto the green end.

Afghan Stitch Coaster

It's a small thing but a coaster can go a long way and makes for a fun small project and handmade gift. This pattern also features the long single crochet. To do this insert the hook into the stitch, yarn over, and draw a loop through to have two loops on the hook. Yarn over again, draw through both loops on the hook. These are really just regular single stitches but worked in a row that isn't the regular working row.

You need white and green worsted weight wool and a size G Tunisian crochet hook.

Row 1: Use the white wool to chain 14, draw up a loop in the second chain from the hook. Draw up a loop in each remaining chain. Yarn over and draw through the one loop.

Row 2-12: Draw up a loop in each vertical bar to get 14 loops on your hook. Yarn over, draw through one loop.

Don't fasten off right now.

Now to work the border.

Row 1: Use the soft white to chain 1, sc evenly around the entire coaster base (use the pattern sc, chain 1, sc) in each corner stitch. Now you fasten off.

Row 2: Join the green yarn in any stitch you want. Sc in some of the places you placed the single stitches in row one, working the singles as you go. Sc in each sc, with three sc in each corner.

Fasten off and you're done.

One Skein Scarf

Scarves are nice but they can use up a lot of wool. Here's a pattern that uses only one skein of wool. This pattern uses the Tunisian double crochet. Just yarn over, slide the hook from right to left under the post of the stitch, draw up a loop, yarn over, and pull through two.

You need one skein of homespun yarn and a 9mm Afghan hook.

 Start by chaining 15.

Row 1: With one loop on the needle, use a simple stitch across the chain and do your return row.

Row 2: Chain two (this counts as your first double crochet), then double crochet across the row. Then return as before.

Row 3: Repeat row one and two until the scarf is as long as you want it to be. When you're done bind off using sc.

Yes it really is that simple.

Chapter 10 Tunisian crochet

Crocheting is an art practice that has been since the 16th century. Nuns taught it to young students, mostly ladies, and at some point, it became a thing of recognition. It is a needlework technique that requires the use of a hook and a fiber-like rope or any other rope-like crochet thread, yarn, wire, or twine to create fabrics by interlocking these materials. Tunisian crochet is one of the many types of crocheting, and it has been said to be a mixed breed of knitting and crocheting, i.e., it combines the technique of knitting and crocheting to produce exceptional results.

While in knitting, many stitches are left open at the same time, crocheting demands that you close all the stitch before proceeding. Taking these distinctions, Tunisian crochets requires that a row is left open followed by a closed row then an open one and on and on it goes. The outcome is usually extraordinary.

Tunisian crochet is one of those crochets that requires a new set of tools aside from the one for regular crocheting. For instance, you must have a very long hook that would aid you in holding the loops. With the use of the Tunisian crochet, you can combine it with common effects, crochet, and stitches. One major thing about the Tunisian stitches is that it has two pass - forward and reverse pass. In the forward pass, the stitches are picked into the hook while in the reverse pass, you work these stitches off the hook.

While there might still be a sort of confusion on how traditional crochet is different from Tunisian crochet, you must know that the Tunisian crochet is an extension of the traditional crochet. This means that the Tunisian crochet is an advanced class for crocheters who feel the need to improve on their skills. This implies that there are a lot of differences between both of them. Some of these differences include:

1. Tools:

In traditional crocheting, the hook used is just 6cm long. At the first end is a hook while the other is straight. The hook is made of either wood, plastic or aluminum and it has a very user-friendly handle. However, in Tunisian crocheting, the hook is about 11cm to 14 cm long.

There is a knob usually attached to the end of the hook that helps prevent your stitches from falling. From the shaft to the handle, it has a very smooth surface, making it look like the needle used for knitting; however, this one has a hook head rather than a pointed mouth.

2. Construction

Having had a glimpse of the difference between the tools used in both crocheting types, we should know how stitches are constructed. You can only go a stitch at a time, I.e., you can only move to the next a rich after you must have completed one. Once the row is completed, you make a series of chains and then start a new row with the same pattern.

This is different in the Tunisian crochet as you have to begin with your foundational chain; afterward, work right to the left, drawing up your loops across whole the row. You'd use your hook to hold these loops. You'd notice you finish a loop b3fore going to the next I traditional crocheting, but that's not the same in Tunisian crocheting as you work the loops across the row to the left side.

3. Fabrics.

It would be difficult to notice any difference in the fabric used in traditional crocheting and Tunisian crocheting if you are starting. You might think Tunisian crochet as weaving or knitting if you see the outcome of Tunisian crochet.

However, you can carry out a litmus test by making a swatch using both techniques, with the same yarn, hook and you'd see that there is an obvious difference between both of them. In the traditional crochet, the fabric has a lot stretch both horizontally and vertically. However, in the Tunisian crochet, there are no stretches horizontally but a lot of stretches vertically. This is possible as a result of the created bars from the return pass.

Also, the edges in Tunisian crochet is even smoother and neater than those of the traditional crochet. While their differences are clear, it is not to show which is better but to show how both can work together.

Getting Started

Once you get the basics of Tunisian crochet like every other craft there is, you get to see how easy it can be. The truth about it is that you would always get better if you practice the more. There are three basic stitches in the Tunisian crochet which include the simple stitches, knit stitches, and purl stitches.

The same way you cannot build a good house without a solid foundation is the same way you cannot execute a Tunisian crochet project without a foundation row and that is where we would begin.

The Foundational Row And The Forward Pass

Here, you make as many stitches of chain and slip knot as you like using the yarn and hook. Afterward, turn the chain to have a good view of the back stitches rather than work on the frontal loop of the chain.

Once the back bump is visible, put your hook under the back stitches of the 2nd chain counting from the hook, then you twist the yarn to pull a loop up. Follow the same process till the last chain.

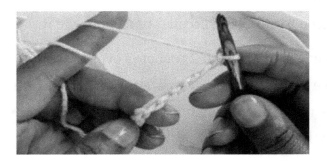

1. Turn the chain to see the back bump

2. Put the hook into the bump on the back of the 2nd chain counting from where the hook is. Pull a loop up

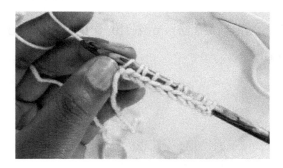

3. Follow the process until the loops are equivalent to the chains

The big deal about the Tunisian crochet is the forward and reverse pass. After the forward pass, you have the reverse pass. Remember we have our loops on the hooks in the forward pass? Now, the reverse pass is simply taking these loops off the hook.

Your first chain, which involves that you yarn it and pull through the 1st loop on the hook, should always be the starting point for your reverse pass. This is so that you can maintain the project's hand. Afterward, pull the loops out of the hook by yarning and pulling it through the following two loops on the hook. Repeat this till you have just a loop on the hook

1. First chain: yarn and pull through the 1st loop on the hook

2. Yarn and pull through the following two loops on the hook

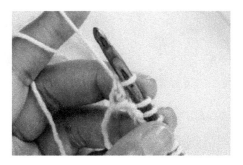

3. Repeat this till you have just a loop on the hook

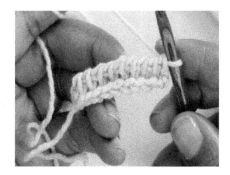

After we must have set the ball rolling with the foundation row, we move to the next which is the knit stitches.

Knit Stitches And The Forward Pass

The knit stitch begins by you identifying the stitch that you would be working into. You'd recall there is an outstanding loop on the hook, yeah? Now, this loop is what you'd use to begin the first stitch. This time, rather than start with the stitch on the right, locate the second stitch and put in your hook in between it's two vertical bars.

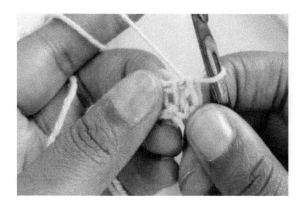

1. Put the hook in between the two vertical bars of the 2nd stitch

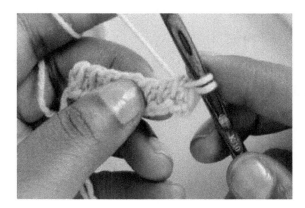

2. Yarn and pull out a loop

3. Follow through the process till the end of the row and stop with just a stitch left.

The final stitch here is quite tricky as you could get it all rough if you are not careful. To ensure it is neat, hold the project at the end with your forefinger and thumb then rotate stitch in between both fingers. Put the hook inside the two loops of the final stitch. Yarn and pull out a loop of finish the stitch.

Knit Stitches and the reverse pass

Follow through the reverse pass of the knit stitch the same way we did it in the foundation row. Start with the first chain, yarn and pull two loops. Repeat it till one loop remains on the hook. The forward and reverse pass of the knit stitch can be continued to whatever length you so desire.

Finishing or Binding

The essence of binding is to secure your stitches and to leave a neat edge. To achieve this, put your hook in between the vertical bars of the preceding stitch like you've done. This time, you don't continue but rather yarn and pull a loop. Afterward, pull through the loop that is on the hook, completing the slip stitch and securing the stitch.

Do this for the whole row. In the end, leave a long tail of the yarn then cut it off. Weave the tail in and out of the project.

Having learned this, we can now proceed to learn other stitch and some other projects.

Basic Tunisian Crochet Stitches

The Tunisian crochet has a lot of stitches, more than you can imagine. However, there are some basic stitches you should be familiar with before you can go advanced. Tunisian basic stitches can look almost alike to a novice but really, there are slight variations between them, and that is where to insert your hook. That is, what makes these stitches different is where and how the hook is inserted.

Using the traditional crochet as an example, you'd recall that we insert our hook through the loop; however, in Tunisian crochet, we work our hook through the bars. Some Tunisian crochet stitches are worked through the horizontal bars; although, most of them are through the vertical. Since we have used the knit stitch on to explain our foundation row and binding, there would be no need to discuss it in details again.

1. The Simple Tunisian Stitch

Trust me when I say that the Simple Tunisian stitch is not like the knitting or other crochet stitches you'd have come across. It is the easiest Tunisian crochet stitch. Imagine the irony. It is called simple stitch because it is the first stitch a beginner must know in Tunisian crochet. It is best used for projects like cowls, headband, etc., as it is good for making thick fabrics that provides a lot of warmth. The firmness of the fabric is dependent on the hook and yarn you use.

This stitch is very easy and straight to the point, and as such, it gives a lot of room for the experimentation of textures and colors. The Simple Tunisian stitch is done by:

a) Put the hook into the vertical bar of the next stitch from right to left

b) Yarn and pull a loop

c) Leave loop on the hook and repeat the process until the end of the row. After you are done with the forward pass, do the reverse pass like it was explained.

2. Tunisian Reverse Stitch

This is much like the Simple Tunisian stitch just that it is in the reverse like the name suggest. Here, rather than work from the front, it is done from the back. You might have to have perfected the Simple Tunisian stitch to get this right. There is this ridge that the Tunisian Reverse Stitch adds to your work. It's best if you want to spice the texture of your work and also if you want to add different colors. The reverse stitch is done by

a) Put the hook into the vertical bar from the back of the next stitch from the right side to the left side.

b) Yarn and pull a loop

c) Leave loop on hook and carry out the process to the end of the row. Afterward, do the reverse pass.

3. Tunisian Knit Stitch

You'd recall that the Tunisian crochet is a mix of knitting and crocheting and yes, there is a Tunisian stitch that is called the Tunisian Knit Stitch that will make your project look like it was purely knitted.

Here, the front of the project which you use the Tunisian Knit stitch is very similar to the stockinet stitch while knitting but when you turn it to the back, you'd see the difference between knitting and Tunisian crochet. You can use this stitch to make anything be it accessories or garments etc.

4. Tunisian Purl Stitch

The Tunisian Purl Stitch looks a lot like the Tunisian Reverse Stitch if you use color. However, you'd be able to spot the difference if you use multiple colors. This means you'd enjoy the outcome of your project better if you make use of multiple colors.

The Tunisian Purl Stitch is a little difficult than the other stitches listed above because of how much swinging it would take to put your hook in and out the stitches. Once perfected, you can make a genius. The Tunisian Purl Stitch is done by:

a) Bringing the yarn to the front, put in the hook from the right side to the left side at the back of the frontal vertical bar of the next stitch.

b) Yarn and pull the loop

c) Leave loop on hook and repeat the process to the end of the row. Afterward, do the reverse pass.

5. Tunisian 2 by 2 Rib

Only a professional knitter can be able to tell the difference between a Tunisian crochet rib and the knitted one. Aside from that, no one else can tell you if your two by two rib was from knitting or Tunisian crochet. It is a combination of Simple Tunisian Stitch and Simple Twisted Stitch to create a spectacular project. Here, alternate both stitches, i.e., if you use the Simple Tunisian stitch now, the next would be the simple twisted stitch, and there you go till the end.

Some other Tunisian crochet stitches include:

6. Tunisian Double Crochet Stitch

You should not be surprised that Tunisian crochet have similar names with the traditional crochet stitches as every stitch in the traditional crochet can be recreated in the Tunisian crochet. Tunisian Double Crochet Stitch is used when you don't want to do a solid project. Here, the stitches are more open and taller than other stitches.

7. Tunisian full stitch

Tunisian full stitched projects are usually very fluffy and attract the hands to it a lot. I would advise you don't use white yarns so as not to get it easily dirty due to the number of touching it would get.

This stitch is more woven than the other stitches and has the texture at the front different from that at the back. You can use it to make scarves and other objects that are reversible.

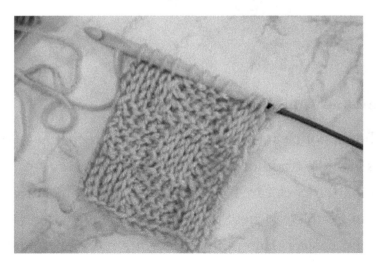

8. Tunisian Basket Weave stitch

Here, your project would have a texture like a basket weave. It is also a common stitch in crocheting and knitting. All you need to do here is to alternate the Tunisian Knit Stitch with the Tunisian Purl Stitch in blocks to create that pattern.

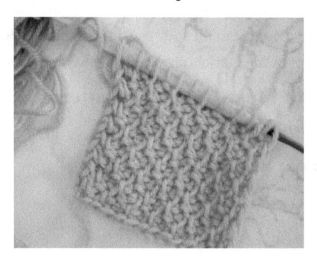

9. Tunisian Honeycomb Stitch

This stitch produces a surface that is lace-like and looks like a honeycomb. Here, Tunisian Knit Stitch with the Tunisian Purl Stitch is used.

Chapter 11 Crochet mandala

Crochet craft is beneficial for everyone because it can improve your overall health and decrease your stress and tensions. You can learn the basic stitches of crochet to prepare these patterns easily. Crochet craft can fill your pocket with money because you can sell them in the market physically or via online stores.

Sample of Most Gorgeous Patterns with Easy Instructions

Pattern 01: Blooming Mandala

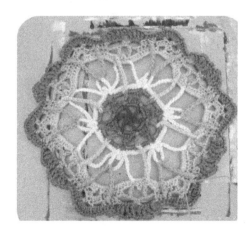

Crochet Hook: 5mm or H/8

Weight of Yarn: (4) Aran and Worsted/Medium Weight (16 to 20 stitches to four inches)

Final Size: 12.5 to 13.5 inches

Notes:

- You will work in rounds with sl st (slip stitch) in the first stitch from the final stitch.

- You should learn to create slip knot on your hook.

- In some rows, the chain 1 will not be taken as a stitch.

- You will use nine colors in this pattern, and you are free to reduce them or use them all. You can repeat a few colors.

- Block the finish items and wet block can be a good choice for this.

- There is no need to fasten off any color until you are satisfied with the row.

- Monitor your stitches with any stitch counter.

Description:

Round 1: Color 1: Create a magic circle, ch 1, single crochet six times into the circle, slip stitch into the first st to secure – 6 single crochets

Round 2: Ch 7 (counts as treble + 3), *treble into the subsequent st, ch 3,* replicate from * to * 4 more times, slip stitch into the top of the ch 4 to secure – 6 trebles, six ch-3 spaces

Fasten off Color 1.

Round 3: Color 2: Create a slip knot on your hook, single crochet into a ch-3 space, single crochet 3 more times into the similar ch-

3 space, ch 1, skip the subsequent treble, *single crochet 4 times into the following ch-3 space, ch 1, skip the subsequent treble,* replicate from * to * 4 more times, slip stitch into the first st to secure – 24 single crochets, 6 ch-1 spaces

Round 4: Ch 2 (counts as the first leg of the double-crochet4together), double-crochet3together the subsequent 3 sts, skip the subsequent ch 1 space, ch 8, *double-crochet4together the subsequent 4 sts, skip the subsequent ch 1 space, ch 8,* replicate from * to * 4 more times, slip stitch into the top of the double-crochet3together to secure – 6 double-crochet4togethers, 6 ch-8 spaces

Fasten off Color 2.

Round 5: 3rd color: Create a slip knot on your hook, single crochet 4 times into a ch-8 space, double-treble into the ch-1 space from round 2, single crochet 4 times into the similar ch-8 space, ch 3, skip the subsequent double-crochet4together, *[single crochet 4 times, double-treble (double-treble) into the ch-1 space from round 2, single crochet 4 times] into the subsequent ch-8 space, ch 3, skip the later double-crochet4together,* replicate from * to * 4 more times, slip stitch into the first st to secure – 48 single crochets, 6 double-treble, 6 ch-3 spaces

Fasten off 3rd color.

Round 6: 4th color: Ch 1, single crochet into the similar st as join, single crochet into the subsequent 8 sts (this includes both single crochet and double-treble), [2 single crochet, picot, 2 single crochet] into the following ch-3 space, *single crochet into the subsequent 9 sts, [2 single crochet, picot, 2 single crochet] into the subsequent ch-3 space,* replicate from * to * 4 more times, slip stitch into the first st to secure − 78 single crochets, 6 picots

Tie-up 4th color.

Round 7: 5th Color: Create a slip knot on your hook, spike single crochet around the first single crochet of the subsequent [2 single crochet, picot, 2 single crochet] in a ch-3 space, ch 10, spike single crochet around the last single crochet of the similar [2 single crochet, picot, 2 single crochet], ch 20, *spike single crochet spike single crochet around the first single crochet of the subsequent [2 single crochet, picot, 2 single crochet] in a ch-3 space, ch 10, spike single crochet around the last single crochet of the similar [2 single crochet, picot, 2 single crochet], ch 20,* replicate from * to * 4 more times, slip stitch into the first spike single crochet to secure − 12 spike single crochets, 6 ch-10 spaces, 6 ch-20 spaces

Tie up 5th color.

Round 8: 6th color: Create a slip knot on your hook, single crochet into a ch 20 space, single crochet 4 more times, ch 15, skip the subsequent [spike single crochet, ch-10, spike single crochet], *single crochet 5 times into the subsequent ch-20 space, ch 15, skip the subsequent [spike single crochet, ch-10, spike single crochet],*replicate from * to * 4 more times, slip stitch into the first st to secure – 30 single crochets, 6 ch-15 spaces

Round 9: Ch 1, single crochet into the similar st as join, single crochet into the subsequent st, picot, skip the subsequent st, single crochet into the subsequent 2 stitches, front post SeptTreble around the subsequent double-treble from round 5, [10 half-double-crochet, ch 5, 10 half-double-crochet] into the subsequent ch-20 space, *single crochet into the subsequent 2 sts, picot, skip the subsequent st, single crochet into the subsequent 2 sts, front post SeptTreble around the subsequent double-treble from round 5, [10 half-double-crochet, ch 5, 10 half-double-crochet] into the subsequent ch-20 space,* replicate from * to * 4 more times, slip stitch into the first st to secure – 24 single crochets, 6 picots, 6 ch-5 spaces, 6 SeptTrebles (septule-treble-crochet), 120 half-double-crochets

Tie up 6th color.

Round 10: 7th color: Pull up a loop in the first single crochet of a [2 single crochet, picot, 2 single crochet], ch 7 (counts as a treble and a ch 3 space), skip the subsequent [single crochet, picot, single crochet], treble into the subsequent st, ch 2, omit the subsequent 4 sts, half-double-crochet into the subsequent 5 sts, skip the subsequent 2 sts, half-double-crochet 6 times into the subsequent ch-5 space, skip the subsequent 2 sts, half-double-crochet into the subsequent 5 sts, ch 2, skip the subsequent 3 sts, *treble into the subsequent single crochet, ch 3, skip the subsequent [single crochet, picot, single crochet], treble into the subsequent st, ch 2, skip the subsequent 4 sts, half-double-crochet into the subsequent 5 sts, skip the subsequent 2 sts, half-double-crochet 6 times into the subsequent ch-5 space, skip the subsequent 2 sts, half-double-crochet into the subsequent 5 sts, ch 2, skip the subsequent 3 sts,* replicate from * to * 4 more times, slip stitch into the 4th st from the bottom of the original ch-7 to secure – 12 trebles, 96 half-double-crochets, 6 ch-3 spaces, 12 ch-2 spaces

Tie up the 7th color.

Round 11: 8th color: Create a slip knot on your hook, single crochet into a ch-3 space, ch 5, skip the subsequent [treble, ch-2 space, half-double-crochet], half-double-crochet into the subsequent 2 sts, SeptTreble into the ch-10 space from round 7 (skip the corresponding st on the round here and throughout this round), half-double-crochet into the subsequent st, ch 3, skip the subsequent 2 sts, single crochet into the subsequent st, ch 3, single crochet into the subsequent st, ch 3, skip the subsequent 2 sts, half-double-crochet into the subsequent St, SeptTreble into the ch-10 space from round 7, half-double-crochet into the subsequent 2 sts, ch 5, skip the subsequent [half-double-crochet, ch-2, treble], single crochet into the subsequent ch-3 space, ch 5, skip the subsequent [treble, ch-2 space, half-double-crochet], half-double-crochet into the subsequent 2 sts, SeptTreble into the ch-10 space from round 7 (skip the corresponding st on the round here and throughout this round), half-double-crochet into the subsequent st, ch 3, skip the subsequent 2 sts, single crochet into the subsequent st, ch 3, single crochet into the subsequent st, ch 3, skip the subsequent 2 sts, half-double-crochet into the subsequent st, SeptTreble into the ch-10 space from round 7, half-double-crochet into the subsequent 2 sts, ch 5, skip the subsequent [half-double-crochet, ch-2, treble],* replicate from * to * 4 more times, slip stitch into the first st to secure – 18 single crochets, 12 ch-5 spaces, 36 half-double-crochets, 12 SeptTrebles, 18 ch-3 spaces.

Tie up the 8th color.

Round 12: 9th color: Pull up a loop in the ch-5 space left of the first single crochet of the previous round, ch 4 (counts as a treble), [treble, Ch 3, 2 treble] into the similar ch 5 space, ch 2, skip the subsequent half-double-crochet, half-double-crochet into the subsequent 3 sts, double-crochet 3 times into the subsequent ch-3 space, ch 2, skip the subsequent single crochet, double-crochet 7 times into the subsequent ch-3 space, ch 2, skip the subsequent single crochet, double-crochet 3 times into the subsequent ch-3 space, half-double-crochet in the subsequent 3 sts, ch 2, skip the subsequent half-double-crochet, [2 treble, ch 3, 2 treble] into the subsequent ch-5 space, ch 2, skip the subsequent single crochet, *[2 treble, ch 3, 2 treble] into the subsequent ch-5 space, ch 2, skip the subsequent half-double-crochet, half-double-crochet into the subsequent 3 sts, double-crochet 3 times into the subsequent ch-3 space, ch 2, skip the subsequent single crochet, double-crochet 7 times into the subsequent ch-3 space, ch 2, skip the subsequent single crochet, double-crochet 3 times into the subsequent ch-3 space, half-double-crochet in the subsequent 3 sts, ch 2, skip the subsequent half-double-crochet, [2 treble, ch 3, 2 treble] into the subsequent ch-5 space, ch 2, skip the subsequent single crochet,* replicate from * to * 4 more times, slip stitch into the top of the original ch-4 to secure -48 trebles, 12 ch-3 spaces, 30 ch-2 spaces, 18 half-double-crochets, 78 double-crochets

Tie-up 9th color.

Carefully weave all ends.

Pattern 02: Flower Madala

Crochet Hook: 6.5mm or K/10.5

Weight of Yarn: Bulky Yarn (5) (12 to 15 stitches for four inches)

Round 1: With the first color, chain 2. Work 10 half-double-crochet in 2nd chain from hook. Join. (10 stitches)

Round 2: ch 1. Work 2 single crochet in each st around. Join. (20 stitches)

Round 3: chain 1. *Work 3 double crochet in subsequent st. Skip 1 st*. Replicate (*) around. Join. (30 stitches, or ten "clusters")

Round 4: ch 1. Working between the clusters for this round, *double crochet, three treble crochet, double crochet*. Replicate (*) around. Join. (50 stitches)

Round 5: Slip stitches over to the 2nd treble crochet. Chain 1. Single crochet in top of center treble crochet. Chain 5. *Skip subsequent four stitches. Single crochet in top of subsequent center treble crochet. Ch 5*. Replicate (*) around. Join. (10 stitches + 10 chain 5 spaces)

Round 6: ch 1. *Single crochet in single crochet st. Work {2 double crochet, treble crochet, ch 1. slip stitch in top of treble crochet just worked, treble crochet, two double crochet} in subsequent chain five space*. Replicate (*) around. Join. Tie-up and weave all ends.

Chapter 12 Techniques and Stitches

There are many more advanced techniques and stitches which can make your crocheting projects much more aesthetically pleasing and fun to create.

Techniques

- **Yarn over Hook**

Wrapping the yarn over your crochet hook is called Yarn Over – or Yo – and it's the most basic step to every crochet stitch. That being said, it must be done right or you won't be able to draw the yarn smoothly onto the next stitch. To do this, you need to:

1. Slide your slip knot to the shaft of your hook.

2. With your yarn hand, hold the tail of the slip knot between your thumb and middle finger.

3. Using the forefinger on your yarn hand, bring the yarn up behind the hook.

4. Lay the yarn over the shaft, positioned between the slip knot and the throat of the hook.

- **Double Strands**

Some patterns will instruct you to work with two strands of yarn at once; these can be two of the same color, or two different. All you would need to do to achieve this, is to use both strands to create your slip knot and then continue to treat both strands as one while you work.

- **Increases and Decreases**

To increase – or *inc* – in crochet, you simply work in more than one stitch, as specified by the pattern, into the same hole. This will increase the number of stitches in the current row you're working on in comparison to the previous row.

To decrease – or *dec* – you work in the first stitch as specified, skipping the final step of the stitch. This is the part where you draw a final loop through the loops on your hook, which leaves the worked loops on the crochet hook, before moving onto the next stitch. When you have completed the second stitch, you'll draw the yarn through all of the stitches on your hook, to draw the first and second stitch together, leaving you with less stitches in the current row in comparison to the previous row.

- **Changing Colors**

Once you have started crocheting, there will be a point in which you'll want to change the color of the yarn you're using. To do this, you need to:

1. Start the work in color A.

2. When you're at the point that you wish to change, work as far as the last single stitch in the row or round, but leave the final stitch unfinished.

3. Grab color B with your crochet hook.

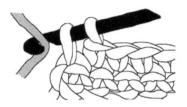

4. Pull up a loop with color B. You may need to gently tug the yarn of color A to keep the loops from getting too big.

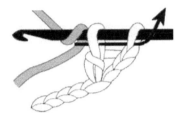

5. You then need to decide whether or not to cut color A. If you're going to use it again within the next few rows, it is better leave as it is, but if not then you'll want to cut the yarn with approximately six inches to spare, which you'll weave in later.

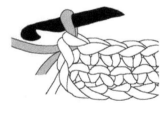

- **Working in the Round**

To begin a crochet pattern that works in rounds, you first need to create the centre ring and crochet the first round. After you complete the number of stitches needed in the first round, join the first and last stitches to complete the circle. Here are the steps to do this:

1. Chain 6 stitches then insert your hook into the first chain stitch you made, forming a ring.

2. Draw the yarn over your hook, then pull it through the stitch and loop it onto your hook, completing your centre ring.

3. Chain 1 stitch, making the turning chain for a single crochet.

4. Insert your hook into the centre ring.

5. Yarn over your hook and draw the yarn through the centre ring.

6. Yarn over your hook and draw the yarn through the 2 loops on your hook.

7. Continue to work single crochet stitches into the ring until you cannot fit anymore.

8. Insert your hook under the 2 top loops of the first single crochet stitch you made.

9. Yarn over your hook and draw the yarn through the stitch and the loop on your hook to complete a slip stitch.

10. Chain 3 stitches to create the turning chain.

11. Work 1 double crochet stitch under the top 2 loops of the first stitch, the stitch directly below the turning chain. Remember, you do not need to turn your work.

12. Work 2 double crochet stitches into each stitch around, then join the first and the last stitch of the round with a slip stitch, completing the round.

- **Making Cords**

A cord has multiple purposes, and is often thought of as something you knit, but as you can see from the direction below, you can also use crochet to create one.

1. Take two long lengths of yarn and double them over.

2. Make a slip knot on your crochet hook with both these pieces of yarn.

3. To make the first stitch of your cord, pull the first loop through the second.

4. Alternating yarn, continue to pull the opposite yarn through the loop on the hook. This will start to resemble a cord as you go.

5. To finish, pull one of the yarn pieces all the way through the opposite loop. Pull the yarn tight and secure and tie two knots for each strand.

• **Joining Yarn**

This is an important step in crocheting, because if you reach the end of a ball of yarn, but need to continue the project, you want this to be seamless to not spoil the appearance of your work. To do this, follow these steps:

1. Double crochet across the row, stopping before the last stitch of the row.

2. Work the last double crochet stitch to the point where 2 loops are left on the hook.

3. Wrap the end of the new yarn around the hook, from back to front.

4. Draw the new yarn through the 2 loops on your hook.

5. Tug on the dropped end of the old yarn at the base of the double crochet to tighten up the stitch.

6. Remove the loop from your hook.

7. Insert your hook into the top of the last double crochet down through the centre of the stitch.

8. Yarn over using the end of the old yarn at the bottom of the stitch.

9. Draw the tail end up through the stitch.

10. Stick your hook back through the hoop to begin your next row.

- **Sewing Together**

A great way to join crocheted pieces together is by using a technique called the whip stitch.

1. Align the pieces you'd like to join together.

2. Weave the yarn back and forth through several stitches on one of the pieces to secure the end. Remember to match the yarn to the pieces you're joining for a better effect.

3. Insert the needle and pull the yarn through the inside loops of the first 2 corresponding stitches of the pieces to be joined. Pull the yarn tight enough to join the pieces, but not too tight, distorting the pieces.

4. Draw the yarn up and over the 2 loops of the first stitch.

5. Repeat the last step through the entire edges to be joined.

6. At the end of the seam, weave the yarn back and forth through several stitches to secure.

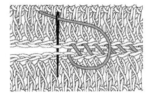

- **Sewing on Buttons**

There are many reasons you may wish to add buttons onto a crocheted project. Whether it's for decoration or practicality, the way you administer them is the same:

1. Use a thread that matches your crocheted project.

2. With the back side of your project facing you, slip your needle through a few of the crocheted chains.

3. Pull the thread through until the tail is almost gone and wrap the thread around a single strand of yarn a few times to secure it.

4. Pull your needle through the project to the front in the position that you wish to attach your button.

5. Sew the thread through the button and the project a few times to secure it.

6. Finish at the back of your project, repeating step 3 to secure the button.

- **Making Pom Poms**

Pom Poms are very simple to make, and are a great addition to a crochet project. To create a pom pom, follow the instructions below:

1. Continuously wrap the yarn around 3 of your fingers, approximately 100 times.

2. Gently slide the bundle of yarn off of your hand.

3. With the same colored yarn, tie the bundle together in the middle.

4. Cut all of the loops on the yarn and trim the shape as desired.

5. You can then sew this to your project using a needle.

If you want to increase or decrease the size of the pom pom, use a different number of fingers and wrap it round less or more times. Pom poms are very simple to create and the more you make, the better you will get at making them.

Stitches

- **Making Ridges**

Ridges can be crocheted for a number of reasons; to add detail to a design, to finish something off nicely or even to give a textured effect. To do this, you need to:

1. Make your Slip Knot stitch and create your foundation chain.

2. Start with a double crochet stitch and repeat this along the row.

3. Don't turn your work; instead work in single crochet stitches from left to right.

4. Create a slip stitch in the turn chain to end this row.

5. Chain 3 stitches and skip the first stitch to create a double crochet stitch in the back loop of the second stitch away from the hook.

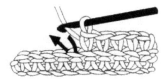

6. Repeat these steps until you have the ridge that you desire.

- **Shell Borders**

Shell borders are very popular as they give a crochet project a pretty edge, without being too fussy or difficult to do. To crochet a shell stitch:

1. Make a slip knot and crochet your foundation chain.

2. Work in a single crochet stitch into the second chain from your hook.

3. Skip the next two chain stitches, then work in a double crochet stitch into the next chin after that.

4. Work four more double crochet stitches into the same chain stitch, completing five double chain stitches.

5. Skip the next two chain stitches, then work a single crochet stitch in the next chain after that.

6. Skip the next two chain stitches and start over again.

- **Forming Picots**

The picot stitch is usually used as edging and added onto a finished garment. You can either start along the edge of something you have already created, or begin by creating a foundation chain of stitches.

1. Single crochet in the first stitch, then chain 3 stitches and single crochet in the next stitch.

2. Single crochet in the next 3 stitches.

3. Chain 3 and single crochet in the next stitch – forming the picot.

4. Repeat steps 2 and 3 until you reach the end of your work to create a chain.

Making different shapes

The possibilities when crocheting are endless, and shapes are a good place to start as they are simple, but very good practice for getting to grips with the basics. Below are the details for how to create some basic crochet shapes.

- **Circle**

1. Start by working a round.

2. Work 2 stitches into each stitch of the previous round.

3. Work 1 stitch into the next stitch, then 2 stitches into the next stitch all around, ending each round with a slip stitch.

4. Repeat step 3 until the desired size is achieved.

- **Square**

1. Make a slip knot and create your foundation chain.

2. Create a half double crochet stitch.

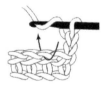

3. Create a single crochet stitch in every stitch along the rest of the row.

4. Turn your work at the end of the row and repeat steps 2 and 3.

5. Repeat step 4 until the square is complete.

- **Triangle**

1. Make a slip knot and create 1 chain stitch.

2. Turn your work and increase 1 stitch at the beginning and end of the row.

3. Repeat step 2 until the triangle is complete.

- **Crochet Flowers**

A flower can be a great accessory added to a garment or household project. To crochet a flower, you need to:

1. Make a slip knot and create a foundation chain of 6 stitches.

2. Use a slip stitch to tie up the ends of the chain, creating a circular shape. This counts as your first double crochet stitch and will be the base for the petals.

3. Make 14 double crochet stitches into the loop, forming the next ring.

4. Make a slip stitch in the first chain of 3, joining the second circle.

5. Create a half double crochet stitch into the first stitch.

6. Make a double crochet stitch and a triple crochet stitch into this first stitch, which will start to give your first petal shape.

7. In the next stitch, create a treble crochet stitch, a double crochet stitch and a half double crochet stitch which will round off your petal.

8. Make a slip stitch in the next stitch.

9. Repeat steps 4 to 8 until you have 5 petals.

- **Stitches in Reverse**

The reverse stitch is sometimes referred to as a crab stitch which creates a twisted, rounded edge that's great for finishing off a project. It's done like this:

1. Insert your crochet hook from front to back, in the next stitch to the right. Be sure to have the right side of your work facing you.

2. Yarn over and draw the yarn through the stitch in a similar way to how you do a single crochet stitch – just in reverse.

3. Yarn over and draw the yarn through the 2 loops on your hook completing one single reverse crochet stitch.

- **Cluster Stitch**

The cluster stitch is made up of a number of stitches that are half closed, then joined together as described below.

1. Make a slip knot and create your foundation chain.

2. Yarn over hook, insert hook into the next stitch.

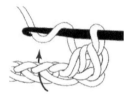

3. Yarn over, draw yarn through the stitch.

4. Yarn over, draw through 2 loops on the hook.

5. Repeat steps 2 to 4 three times.

6. Yarn over and draw through the 5 loops on the hook. This completes a cluster created with 4 double crochet stitches.

Chapter 13 Choosing a Crochet Pattern

Choosing a crochet pattern is indeed a very difficult one because there are several crochet patterns here.

But doing this thing is so easy, and you do not need to learn more and try more just to create this one. When you are good in arts, that would be the advantage for you because in doing these such things, you need to be more creative and more artistic. The purpose of which is for you to be able to create a beautiful one and also it may be the result of a good product.

If you really want to create this, you need to learn the basic patters. You may use social media most especially the YouTube for you to watch the video tutorial of creating these patterns as well as choosing a pattern of crochet patterns. There are videos out there that will help you to do those different patterns or designs. If you are going to create a bag, there is a pattern that you will use, or you will be as your guide for you to achieve the bag that you really want to do.

If you prefer to create this one, make sure that you have some materials that is needed when you are about to do this most especially the important one the yarn because yarn serves as a basic foundation of everything most especially in crochet and of course when you are using yarn be sure that you have the combination of light color and dark yellow for the contrast and to make it more a better one.

Different Types Of Yarns You Can Find, And You May Use In Your Crochet

Nowadays there are different types of yarns in the market and you as a customer you deserved to get the yarn that you really want and make sure that you will pick the smooth one. Those yarns are good to create and make a crochet. As a new creator of those designs, you have the right to get the better one. You also have the right to complain if you are not satisfied with the yarn that you bought in the market specifically in a company or store that sells fiber and yarns. The best yarn that you are going to use especially when you are a newbie it should be in a smooth texture and contains cotton for you to be able to create more and more. Secondly, the crochet hook, this is also an important thing when you are creating a crochet because this serves as your guide to be in your correct pathway. When you will buy this kind of crochet hook make sure that you will check the size, but you need to check if your crochet hook will use in yarns because some crochet hooks are needed and used in threads especially when you will choose a small size of the crochet hook.

How Social Media Can Help You With Your Crochet Patterns

As you can see on the social media especially in everything that is considered as a good site, you can see that there are several types of crochet hook that is made of aluminum, plastic, ceramic, and etc. You need to start in simple designs and patterns for you to be able to upgrade more if there is something wrong with what will be in your product on your first entry. It is really okay if you did something wrong in your first try because the first try would not be that perfect as you wanted, but this might be the best for you to learn from what you have been doing in your first try. And if that is the case, your first try would be your motivation and inspiration for you to improve more of your preferred designs in your crochet patterns.

Considering The Proper Way Of Holding The Crochet Needle

If you also wanted to make this or try this, you will also check in your preferred way of holding the crochet hook because if you would not hold this in a proper way, you will be in accident or incident. If you are left-handed person make sure that you will hold the crochet hook in your left hand and if you also a right-handed person be sure that you will hold this crochet design with your right hand. As you can see in your community, there are people using this crochet because this is the best way to create something new and this will teach you how to innovate just like t-shirts, undershirt, cap, wallets and other products that are made up of yarns. If you are going to make those things try to explore on the social media especially in the YouTube and Google using your mobile phones, androids, iPhone and other gadgets try to search and explore because this will help you to make your task simpler and easy to finish.

Common Crochet Designs

Choosing a crochet pattern is a hard thing to do because it is really hard to choose what might be the chosen designs like flowers, butterflies, design and etc. But if you can see in your market the most common design that you will see is flower because it is a convenient one and easy to do most especially when you will your mobiles to search on the internet. There are several techniques that will be going to use, and you will find out that if you are going to search on the googles. Yarn and crochet hook are a basic foundation of this item because without the Yarn and crochet hook, this would not be a very beautiful one and this may not result in an item.

Choosing a crochet patterns is indeed worth it because at the end of the day your preferred design would be your design in your item just like for example you are torn between the butterfly design or the flower design you will pick in that two choices of what design you really want to design in your shirt and for example you chose the flower design, of course, you will be used the flower design as your design in your shirts, and you will also follow the patterns. There are three types of yarn. These are Ball, Skein, and Hank. The Ball is round and covered up in a ball, Skein is just like a Ball, but skein is an oval shape, and also the Hank has a twisted shape.

When you are choosing what kind of yarn you will be using, make sure that you know the weights of your preferred yarn. If you browse some of the pattern on the internet you will know that there are different patterns like a scarf, cardigan, hat, jacket, baby hoodie jacket, blanket, baby hat, pillow set and etc. Scarf pattern can be placed at your shoulder, and it can be used as a cover when you feel cold. Cardigan pattern is very similar to jacket at it also used when you feel cold at night. Hat pattern serves as your protection on your head in times of sunny days. The jacket is very similar to a scarf and cardigan when it comes to their functions and uses it can also use in a cold weather because it will help you to cover your skin. Baby hoodie jacket pattern will help the babies to cover their skin as well as their body in a cold weather. The blanket pattern is used as your cover when you are sleeping. The baby hat pattern is used by babies to protect their head from sun and heat. Pillow set pattern is used to cover your pillow, and it makes your pillow more presentable and beautiful. These patterns will help you to create such things, but there are some patterns that did not mention here. Some people love to do these things because doing these things helps them to relieve their sadness, madness, and boringness. So, if you really wanted to make and create this you are free from choosing the designs as well as the patterns you wanted to do. If someone wanted to create this and make this, of course, you would lend your time to teach them because sharing is caring and it is not bad to share your ideas and learning to someone who is eager to learn.

When you choose a design, it is really hard to decide what will be your design because there are different kinds of patterns and designs that exist today. But then again, your choices matter most today and you need to consider the designs that you really wanted to do. Consider the designs and patterns that you really wanted because at the end of the day if you did something that you never wanted you will not be satisfied at all. So, please choose your chosen design or patter for you to be able to satisfy on what you are doing.

If you are planning to sell those things you did of course you might consider your target market if it is student you might sell your product in a lower price because your customer is a student only and they have their own priorities. And when it is adult, your price would be at least similar to the student's price because some people have also their own priorities. Choosing a crochet pattern, crochet design, usually makes your product more attractive because when you will sell this one you will always consider the design that makes your customer attractive.

Choosing a yarn is always part of creating a crochet pattern. You will not be able to create a beautiful one if you will not consider the type of yarn that you really need to use. How to choose color? Of course, you will choose a color that will compliment on your preferred design. You may look at the color wheel that has color for you to be able to choose the color you wanted to choose.

The best combination to your chosen color would be if you will use the light color the color that would complement to a light color is dark color. Crochet is a complex because in creating a crochet pattern it may consists different colors. When you choose a pattern or design you need a pattern collection for you to be able to have a guidance of your chosen patterns. When you choose a pattern or design you need a Time for you to be able to make into a very successful one and for you to make into a beautiful one. If you wanted to add other designs and patterns you might search on the internet the other designs that you are not really familiar and after searching you need to lend your time to watch the prescribed design. If you wanted too to add other design or patterns you may look on the books for your guidance to create a design that you wanted to explore. Using internet and books is indeed a helpful one because of that reference you will be able to create those designs that are not really familiar to you. You may also search on the internet and find your chosen pattern and design and use your crochet hook to do those things such as jacket, cardinal, hats, blanket, baby jackets, baby hats and etc.

Using internet, you will also be able to explore more of the other patterns that are not familiar to you. Browsing on the internet is a helpful one especially for those people who are first time to create that one and make that one. Indeed, without internet and book what will happen to you? Of course, you will not create a product without any reference unless otherwise you have an idea on the other designs and patterns. Exploring something new is not a bad thing to do. Exploring means you are willing to lend your time to have an idea into something and exploring means you have to do everything just to have new idea and learnings. Exploring about different patterns and designs is not a difficult thing to do yet it is the best way for you to be able to learn new things and learn something that you are not really familiar with.

Commonly used and important materials in doing these things are Yarn and Crochet Hook. Without these materials you will not be able to create those things and without them you will not meet your satisfaction especially to your customer when you are planning to sell these all. Yarn is a very important thing in creating this one because it is a basic unit and it serves as the foundation of crochet. Thread also can be used in creating a crochet it is a substitution for yarn when yarn is not available anymore in the market. Cardboard cut outs are also an important thing especially in creating a tassel. You need to start in simple designs and patterns first for you to be able to make a complex one. Starting in a simple design makes your designs and patterns more complex. Because when will you start in a small idea of course as time passes by your idea would be bigger one and your idea would upgrade to make it big. You as a part of your community of course you will know what you community preferred design and pattern.

Consider your weather as well in that idea your mind would think of the possible pattern that you will make. When it is cold of course you will create a jacket for your customer to cover their body from fog and cold weather. When it is cold you will be able to think of the possible ides for example your community needs a scarf, jackets and cardinal you as a producer you would do those things for you to be able to sustain what is their need and what is their wants. When it is sunny day your mind would think of the possible idea of course you also as a producer you would create and make hats for them to protect their head from sunlight and heat. It is okay for you to lend your time to do this because you will be the one to sustain their need in terms of a weather. You as a creator of a crochet you will be the one to add more ideas and you will be the one who will create new one. It is up to you what would be your preferred design but if your customer requested to you their preferred design of course you will accept their suggestions and after they pick a suggested design and patterns it is your time to create that specific thing.

Your customer's design will always be acceptable because of the end of the day they will be the one who will serve as your boss. It is really hard to decide some of the patterns because as you will browse on the internet and if you will be referred to the books some of the designs and patterns are difficult to do. It has a guide but when you read those guides at the end of the day you will find it difficult. But when you are looking for an idea it is better to search on the internet, it is better ti read of some books and also it is great when you seek or ask help from the people who are doing this before. Seeking and asking help from the people who did this before is an advantage one and it will help you to do it hands on and oral and for those people who will help you will be very much happy because their learning and ideas would be shared to you. Be thankful for those people who are willing to help you because those people will help you to rise up and bring you up not to bring you down and those people are willing to do just to share their learnings. Think of it, some people are selfish when it comes to their idea but there are also some people who will help you and there some people who will extend their willingness just to teach you of some of the important things when designing and you will apply some of the designs that are not very familiar to you. When you are in the first time to do is it okay to be rejected, neglected and ignored by some people. Anyway, being rejected will be the reason for you to be able to pursue what your desired thing to do. Choosing a design and pattern is an easy thing to do because choosing between different patterns and designs is an enjoyable moment yet hardest.

Chapter 14 Crocheting Background

Its origin is however unclear since the skill was mostly been spread verbally between interested parties. They would copy the crochet pattern from someone's original work. This would result in different types of crochet mistakes hence no perfection of any of the styles.

Research states that crocheting may have started in china through their needlework which was a very common practice in Turkey and India as well as in North America. It is after this that the crocheting methods reached Europe but they would refer to it like a tambourine. Tambourine later evolved to 'crocheting in the air' since the fabric used in the background had to be removed in order the stitch to stand on its own.

Crocheted fabrics became popular in Europe in the 19th century. Instructions about crocheting were first published in a magazine in the year 1823. The magazine had detailed information about the color plate which contained different styles. After publishing the magazine, the first crochet patterns were printed in 1824.

Mlle. Riego do la Branchardiere is said to have contributed a lot in the popularity of crocheting in Europe. This is as a result of the patterns books that she published in the 1800s which were so easy to duplicate. The pattern books were given to millions of women who had an interest in crocheting. This was a sure way to ensure that the patterns reached as many women as possible whether they could afford the books or not.

Many women around the world started copying the patterns which made crocheting so popular. There are a lot of materials that one can learn from on the internet. One can, therefore, learn about crocheting from websites and different sites on the internet. Different crochet pattern books have also published which contain different and unique crochet styles. It is therefore evident that crocheting has greatly evolved which has made it so popular. Many modern crocheted clothing is already being sold in our markets worldwide.

What makes one think of crocheting?

Many people around the world have mastered the art of crocheting. This is as a result of the many benefits that come with it. Different people will, however, crochet for different reasons. There are many people out there who may be wondering why people crochet. They do not see enough reason why one should spend their free time crocheting. Most times, they lack the motivation to start crocheting so it would be great if I highlight a few reasons for crocheting.

Crocheting is a stress reliever: Crocheting has been tried and proven to be one of the activities that help people to relieve stress. This is because as you crochet, you can forget all the challenges you may be going through. All your concentration is on the pattern making so all your mind is occupied. As you crochet, all that is in your mind evaporates which helps a lot in relaxing your mind. Whenever one needs to learn a new crocheting skill, they have to go through different books, sites and also apps which normally engage them mindfully. One forgets everything they are going through since they are curious to learn a new skill.

Crocheting brings a great sense of accomplishment: There is no better feeling than seeing people wear or cover themselves with items that you crocheted yourself. It makes you feel great about the time you spent crocheting the items. It isn't a waste of time as you can see them enjoy the fruits of your labor. That feeling is so fulfilling that you will want to keep crocheting. You will also keep on discovering new patterns and after implementing the skill, there will be a great sense of fulfilment.

Crocheting enables you to have an alert mind: People grow older each day. Crocheting offers a lasting solution to people who would want to remain alert as well as stimulated. One has to remain alert especially when they are working on new a new pattern. Isn't it, therefore, important to engage our mind with crocheting?

Keeping the tradition alive: We mostly inherit the crocheting skills from our parents, aunts and even from our grandmothers. It would be a great thing to keep the tradition alive by passing it on to the people around us. It is very important to ensure that we pass down the crocheting art to our children and even people around us. For every crochet, there is some bit of love from the people we learn the art from.

Crocheting keeps you busy: Whenever one is crocheting, their mind is fully engaged. This means that they are busy hence will not be thinking about anything else. Being busy is beneficial in that, one won't be idling around without doing any meaningful thing. For most people, crocheting is a hobby so they use their free time doing it.

Enhancing one's creativity: We learn a new trick every day. Through crocheting, one can perfect their skills by designing new patterns. They can creatively mix different color schemes to come up with beautiful patterns which make the crochets to be more appealing. It is through Crocheting that one can experience a comforting effect from the great textures created through the repeated movements using yarns of different colors.

Health benefit: Apart from relieving stress, crocheting is of great benefit to people suffering from arthritis. This is because as one works through various stitches, the fingers remain nimble hence reduce the risks of arthritis. People who get Alzheimer's attacks are also advised to consider engaging in crocheting. This is because they are able to reduce the attacks by a great percentage. Whenever they engage themselves in learning a new skill, they get to preserve some of the memories they have made in the past.

The Economic part of Crocheting

Many people around the world have been able to learn crocheting skill. It is an industry that has grown and has empowered very many men and women around the world. This has greatly improved the economy. Below are some of the economic impacts of crocheting. Do crotchets have an economic impact? Several people may not find crocheting beneficial. They may not see it as a source of income, but it contributes immensely to the economy.

During cold seasons people look for warm things to keep them warm. They, therefore, have to purchase scarfs, sweaters, socks and other products made from yarn. This increases the rate of yarn production as a result of the increase in demand for crocheted items. This is said to lead to the growth of the economy. Below are some of the economic impacts brought by crocheting.

So many crocheting companies have been opened which has created employment opportunities for many families around the world. They can take care of their families from the income they earn from the crocheting companies.

Women can crochet items and sell them to people in their neighbourhood which enables them to earn some income. This helps to improve the economy since they do not become dependent on the government for their survival. The government is, therefore, able to concentrate on other development projects since its people are not overly dependent on them.

People have also been able to come up with unique patterns and have published them in books which are later sold to interested parties. This acts as a source of income for the publisher which also helps in the growth of the economy.

The experts in this area have also taken up the role of training more people in crocheting. This ensures the empowerment of more people which means more skilled individuals in a country.

Individuals who have specialized in information technology also develop apps which contain crochet instructions. This has helped people to have easy access to the skills so anyone can install the app and learn the skills in their own free time.

Social and Traditional Impact of Crocheting

Crocheting has had a great impact on our society. The skill keeps on being passed on from one generation to another. This has helped a lot in impacting of people's lives socially and even traditionally. Below are some social and traditional impacts brought about by crocheting?

For Charity: Most often, we find ourselves with different types of crotchets which we mostly make during our free time. One can craft some items and give them out for charities. It will always feel great when one benefits from an item crocheted with a lot of love. It will act as a way of showing your generosity and sense of care for others. One will feel good when someone appreciates something that was made purposely to suit their need.

Aesthetic value: Crocheting can display the beauty of a tradition. Before the invention of big companies that dealt with the manufacturing of clothes, people used to wear crocheted clothes. Some people make crochets to beautify the environment. One, therefore, makes items that they are sure that they will make their environment calm. This will enable them to feel relaxed whenever they are around.

Boost self-esteem: We all feel good when complimented for doing something so well. Compliments motivate us to produce better crochets which are better the previous ones. When we sell the crafts we made or give it as a gift, it boosts your self-esteem. You feel great about your accomplishments. Self-esteem can also be built through learning new skills. One can feel productive which creates beauty through self-expression.

Reduces stress and anxiety: We all get stressed up at some point in our life. We may become anxious as a result of the strenuous activities we may have engaged in on our daily activities. One needs to give themselves a break. Getting a yarn and crochet would be of great help in relaxing their mind. It is through the repetition of the stitches as you count the rows that your mind gets some kind of relaxation. All the anxiety thoughts are set free since your focus is on creatively making the crochets.

Eases and relieves depression: Our emotions keep changing depending on the occasion. For instance, in the grieving period, it seems impossible to overcome your grief. Most times we feel like the world has come to an end. Crocheting can be a comforter during the grieving period. Crafting such as crocheting is said to be helpful in the stimulation of dopamine which enables one to feel happier and emotionally stable.

Keeps one busy: Imagine you are left at home alone. No other work for you, you can choose to do some crocheting. You will be relaxing at the same time keeping yourself busy. You don't have to create wonderful products out of it. The whole idea is to keep your mind engaged through a useful course which may help you earn some income or even contribute to charity. In a scenario where you are following up on a program on the television, your hands will be busy crafting while your eyes are glued to the television. The best thing about crocheting is that one can engage every member of the family. They will be able to contribute to various ideas about what you are making and suggestions on colors and even designs.

Brings communities together: There are many ways to bring people together. One of them is having yarn crafting introduced to a community. They can have a meet up in public to do crocheting. The organizers can organize a fiber fair together with related events. This will be of great help since people from different places will be able to meet and share ideas. They will be able to learn from one another hence more creative designs. The community can even come together and build yarn stores which will benefit the community from the sales made in the store. All the participants can also buy the yarn at a reduced price which will enable them to make more crocheted items for sale. They in return become more productive which brings economic empowerment amongst them.

Chapter 15 Benefits of Crocheting

Crocheting is also helpful in reducing physical pain. Rheumatoid arthritis, fibromyalgia, and multiple sclerosis are only some of the chronic pain conditions that you may have. Through crocheting, you can have a positive distraction that takes your mind off the pain that you feel. It also helps release serotonin, which is the natural painkiller in your body. It can even help keep your hands limber in order to reduce the pain caused by arthritis and other similar conditions.

If you are insomnia, crocheting may help you sleep better at night. Likewise, crocheting may help you manage your restless leg syndrome. Oftentimes, anxiety causes you to have difficulty sleeping. If you are anxious all the time, you will not be able to get sufficient rest and sleep. You can start crocheting to keep you busy at night and allow your brain to relax. Crochet patterns with repetitive motions can have a soothing effect on your mind and body. Crocheting can be a form of meditation that can help you sleep.

You have just read that anxiety can cause you to lose valuable sleep. What's more, anxiety can lead to more serious health conditions. Anxiety is, in fact, a by-product of constant worrying. Through crocheting, you can effectively reduce your anxiety levels. This activity is beneficial for different types of anxiety disorders, such as social anxiety, generalized anxiety and panic attacks.

Whenever you find yourself stressing about people or situations, you can start to crochet. If you often get anxious while waiting for test results or other news, crocheting can help relax your mind so you can focus on the important details. Complicated crochet patterns are highly recommended to quiet your restless mind. What's more, research has shown that crocheting is an effective way for coping with pregnancy-related anxiety.

When you have an illness, you can also feel grief. For instance, having an illness that diminishes your functionality can make you feel sad for losing a once productive life. Through crocheting, you can be more productive, creative, and useful, even when you feel that you are losing functionality in certain aspects of your life. Crocheting can also help boost your mood levels, so you can cope with grief more easily. If you do not learn how to overcome it, grief may paralyze you.

In addition, crocheting can unleash your creativity and other hidden talents. Through this activity, you can explore different aspects, such as techniques, colors, shapes, textures, designs, stitch patterns, finishing details and project types. Some people do not even get to finish their crochet projects because they are more interested in the process rather than the outcome.

Likewise, some people start crocheting because of the new knowledge and skill that they will acquire. For them, knowledge is as important as the finished project. Some enthusiasts also aim to pass on their knowledge to other people, as well as inspire them to start crocheting and making crochet projects.

If you have any physical limitations, crocheting can help you overcome them as well. It can challenge your hand-eye coordination in a productive, therapeutic, and manageable way. For those who are blind, crocheting is a great way to develop their other senses further, particularly the sense of touch.

Moreover, crocheting can foster friendship, community, charity and companionship. You can crochet with a group of people who also like the activity. For some people, crocheting is another way to give to charities, organizations and communities that may find their crochet projects useful.

Chapter 16 History of Crochet

Crocheting has been around for centuries. The term crochet originated from the words *croche* or *croc*, which is French for *hook*. It is relaxing, fun and simple enough that even beginners can learn it. It is also an ideal hobby for people who want to create decorative and fashionable projects, including hats, tops, scarves, ponchos, bedspreads, doilies and tablecloths.

You only need two things to crochet: a ball of yarn or thread and a hook. All stitches are created by wrapping the thread or yarn around the hook. At first, you may find it a bit confusing or difficult to do. However, as you continue to do it, the entire process will be easier for you.

Most patterns begin with a series of loops, also called chains, or a slip stitch. Nevertheless, you can easily learn how to create a foundation without using a standard chain. Projects are typically worked in rows wherein you have to stitch back and forth, with every row over the previous row. You can also stitch in rounds wherein you work around a ring of chains and create a geometric figure, such as a circle, hexagon or square. You can also use a motif or a geometric piece to stitch together and form your crochet project.

Annie Potter, world traveler and crochet expert, said that crocheting started in the 16th century. Back then, it was called *chain lace* in England and *crochet lace* in France. In 1916,

Guiana Indians' descendants were visited by Walter Edmund Roth. He found examples of crochet.

Lis Paludan, a writer and researcher from Denmark, had three theories. She said that crochet may have originated in Arabia then spread westwards to Spain and eastwards to Tibet, eventually making its way to Mediterranean countries. She also said that crochet's earliest evidence was found in South America, in which a primitive tribe was claimed to have used crochet adornments during puberty rites. Her third theory states that early forms of crochet, particularly three-dimensional dolls, were found in China.

Paludan added that there aren't any convincing evidence as to how old crochet may be or where it really originated. It was not possible to look for evidence in Europe before the 1800's. A lot of sources also claimed that crochet has already been known as far back as the 1500's. It was called *nun's lace* or *nun's work* in Italy because it was used by nuns for church textiles.

Another theory was that crochet was directly developed from Chinese needlework, which is an ancient form of embroidery known in India, Turkey, North Africa and Persia and has reached Europe in the 1700's. It was actually called the *tambouring*, which came from *tambour*, the French word for drum.

In this method, a frame is used to stretch the background fabric while the working thread is held beneath it. A hook with a needle is inserted and a loop is drawn through the fabric. While the loop is still on the hook, the hook is inserted farther along the fabric and another loop is drawn up to form a chain stitch. Tambour hooks are as thin as needles, which is why very fine thread has to be used.

By the end of the 18th century, tambour evolved into *crochet in the air*. It involved the background fabric being discarded and the stitch working on its own. In the early 1800's, crochet started to become prominent in Europe, especially after being popularized by Mlle. Riego de la Branchardiere, who was known for her talent in taking old designs and turning them into crochet patterns that are easy to copy. She has published a lot of pattern books for women to use. She also claimed to have invented the Irish crochet or lace-like crochet.

The Irish crochet was actually sort of a lifesaver for the Irish people. It delivered them out of the potato famine, which lasted for five years. They sold their crochet work to well-off people abroad. During this time, they had a hard time working and living. So, they crocheted in the day in between chores. When the sun has set, they use candlelight to see their crochet patterns.

However, keeping their crochet projects had been quite a problem for most of them were living in squalor. They did not have a place to store their work. Keeping their crochet projects under their bed only made them dirty. Good thing, these things could be washed. However, most of the buyers from other countries were not aware that their delicate cuffs and collars were made in poor condition.

The Irish workers, including children, men and women, were organized into cooperatives. They formed schools to teach individuals how to crochet. They also trained teachers and sent them to different parts of Ireland so they can teach more people how to crochet. Soon enough, the workers were able to design and create their own crochet patterns.

Even though a lot of people died in less than ten years, they were still able to survive the potato famine. More than one million Irish citizens perished, but many families were still able to make it through, thanks to their crochet projects. The money they made from selling crochet work allowed them to save up and immigrate to other countries. A lot of them actually went to America, taking their crocheting skills with them.

It was believed that two million Irish people went to America between 1845 and 1859 and four million more went there by 1900. The American women were busy with weaving, spinning, quilting and knitting back then, but they were still influenced by the Irish to crochet. This explains why the Americans have also become adept at crocheting.

Crocheted Projects

In the early centuries, it was the men's job to create their own handiwork. Fishermen and hunters, for instance, created knotted strands of cords, strips of cloth, or woven fibers to snare birds or fish and trap animals. They also made fishing nets, knotted game bags and cooking utensils. They created things that have practical uses.

Eventually, they expanded their handiwork to personal décors. They used these things during special occasions, such as celebrations, religious rites, marriages, and funerals. It was common to see ceremonial costumes that featured crochet-like ornamentation as well as decorative trimmings for the wrists, arms and ankles.

During the 16th century, wealthy people and members of the royal family of Europe wore jackets, gowns, headpieces and lace-trimmings. The poor people cannot afford such lavish clothing; hence, they used crochet to make their clothing more attractive. Crochet became their imitation of expensive lace.

Fast forward to the Victorian era, crochet patterns were made for bird cage covers, flower pot holders, card baskets, lamp shades, lamp mats, tablecloths, wastepaper baskets, tobacco pouches, antimacassars, purses, caps, waistcoats, and rugs with foot warmers.

From 1900 until 1930, the women became busy crocheting slumber rugs, Afghans, traveling rugs, sleigh rugs, chaise lounge rugs, car rugs, coffee cozies, teapot cozies, hot water bottle covers, and cushions. During this time, potholders were popularized and became a staple in every repertoire.

During the 1960's until the 1970's, crochet became a free-form way of expression. This is evident in today's 3-dimensional sculptures, clothes, tapestries, and rugs that depict the realistic scenes and abstract designs of yesteryears.

Early Origins and History

We do not know many things regarding the early origins of crochet because the ancient textiles that survived are very few. Some claim that originally, women used fingers to create loops and chains.

Only later did they begin to use a tool very similar to the current hook, which was initially made of wood, bone, or bamboo and then in ivory and amber.

The oldest find, considered a precursor of crochet, comes from Jutland. It is a woolen cap that dates back to about 3100 years ago. However, primitive textile samples were found in every corner of the globe — Far East, Asia, North and South America, and Europe.

Some scholars believe that Tambour work was at the origin of modern crochet. This technique was used in China. It required the use of a fine hook to weave threads through a netted background.

This technique arrived in France around 1720.

An American scholar, Mary Thomas, believes that crochet work originally comes from the Arabian Peninsula. From here it spread eastward, in Tibet, and to the west, in Spain and then, thanks to merchants and sailors, even in other parts of the world.

The most delicate crochet form originated in Italy in the 16th century and was used by the sisters for making ornaments and vestments. It was considered a typical occupation within the monasteries where sisters created precious lace using very thin yarns. The linen for the altars were fitted with crocheted borders not only for decorative purposes, but also to make it more durable. Very soon, it spread to Spain and Ireland, which were very Catholic countries.

Only in the 19th century did crochet begin to be appreciated in the bourgeoisie and the noble. The laces were used to adorn the linen of the house and underwear. Lace, finished with precious scallops full of picots and various decorations, had a huge development especially among the ladies of the bourgeoisie, and they adorned their precious clothes with collars, gaskets and tippets.

The crochet, which until then was not considered a genre in its own right, developed to mimic the difficult points of Venetian lace. The work was faster than needle and bobbin lace and tools were simpler and easier to find.

Perhaps its popularity took off from a lady of French origin, Eleanore Riego de la Branchadière, who settled in Ireland, where she remained impressed by the delicacy of the work of the nuns in a convent in Dublin. She not only perfected their skills, but spoke of the art of crochet in her magazine "The Needle". She also published eleven books in which contained conversion tables from needle lace and bobbin lace to crochet.

She is commonly credited with the invention of the Irish Lace. When times were hard, women had to find ways of supporting their families. This was particularly true during and after the great potato famine of the 1840s, when crochet became the sole economic support. Another factor that contributed to the spread of crochet was the creation of a kind of domestic industry born in Clones to help the poorest families, thanks to Cassandra Hand, the wife of a local parish priest. The Clones Lace, still widely known, is a variant of Venetian lace. The Venetian lace, although very beautiful, required considerable time and Irish women found that by using the crochet hook, they could achieve the same effect in less time. These women reproduced elements linked to their environment: shamrocks, fern, brambles, wild roses, daisies, or star-shaped figures.

When Queen Victoria promoted the crochet lace in an exhibition of Arts in London, fashion took off. Soon, demand became so high that professional sellers took the place of charities and the activity of lace turned from survival activities into an industry. The patterns of crocheted lace began to be written and distributed. Irish girls traveled to other parts of the world to teach crocheted lace.

From the Irish Lace came the Orvieto lace, which, over the years, has acquired a peculiarity and original identity. In 1907, the Ars Wetana, a "patronage for young workers" was born. It sought to carry out the activity of production and packaging of lace and frill with special ornamental details for the Duomo of Orvieto, aimed at strengthening and development of local crafts.

The popularity of crochet reached its peak between 1910 and 1920, with fashion of the Edwardian era. Its models were more complex stitches and the prevalence of white yarn. They began to be printed in series books with crochet patterns that took the place of honor in the decoration and creation of clothes and household items.

In 1930, fashion acquired simpler features. Art Deco was the trend of the moment, and crochet was used primarily for garments of children and infants, christening gowns, gloves, and blankets. During the Second World War, yarn was rationed and since crocheting wastes more yarn than knitting, crochet seemed to be doomed.

Despite the fact that crochet was all the rage in Europe, it hadn't really gained much popularity in America. The majority of women who crocheted were immigrants who loved the availability of ready-made threads and other materials.

After the turn of the century, America finally accepted crochet and it became part of the many skills taught to young girls. It was considered a leisure activity since it did not produce a functional or marketable good. It was pretty much reserved for the middle and upper classes.

In the '60's/crochet came back strongly in vogue after long hibernation, using the vivid colors of granny squares.

Crochet's popularity continued to grow until the '70's, with ponchos being the must-have accessories.

In the '80's, crochet began to fall out of favor. The economy was growing and more women were working, thus having less time for crafts. Plus, crochet work was no longer affordable.

Crochet and knitting lost their importance even in the school curriculum — nobody taught it anymore, and the new generation had no time to learn. This time, it seemed that crochet was really facing extinction.

Fortunately, since the middle of the '90s, crochet has experienced a new period of interest. Crochet can be seen today as a hobby, but for those who have awareness, they consider it an art form.

Chapter 17 Glossary

Abbreviations

Some commonly used abbreviations:

St(s): stitch (es).

Inc = increase

Dec= decrease

Sc= single crochet

Ch= chain

Sl st = slip stitch

Dc: double crochet.

Sk: skip

Hdc: half double crochet.

* or ( ): repeat what is in between the asterisks or parenthesis.

Terms

Crochet has its own vocabulary that you will encounter when you read a crochet pattern. Here are some of the most frequently used terms and abbreviations.

- **Chain stitch, ch.** Basic crochet stitch. These interlocking yarn circles form your first line of crochet.

- **Decrease, dec.** Eliminate one or more stitches.

- **Double Crochet, dc.** One of the basic crochet stitches.

- **Half Double Crochet, hdc.** One of the basic crochet stitches.

- **Increase, inc.** Add one or more stitches.

- **Join.** Join two stitches together, usually using a slip stitch.

- **Single Crochet stitch**, **sc.** Basic crochet stitch. This stitch will connect to the chain stitch. You can make your first project using just the chain and single crochet stitch.

- **Skein.** The yarn you buy comes in a coiled arrangement called a skein. Working from the skein cause tangles. To make your crocheting life simpler, take the time to wrap the yarn into a large ball.

- **Repeat.** Do again.

- **Slip knot.** The beginning stitch in crochet. The initial yarn circle.

- **Slip stitch, sl st.** Used to join the beginning and end of a line.

- **Triple crochet, tr or trc.** Basic crochet stitch.

- **Tunisian Crochet.** This combination of crochet and knitting uses a long crochet hook with a stopper at the end to keep the stitches from falling off the hook.

- **Turn.** Turn your work so you can work back for the next row.

How to Read Crochet Patterns and Terminology

One of the most intimidating parts about learning to crochet is reading the pattern. At first glance, it may seem rather complicated, but as you become familiar with crochet knowledge, you'll soon see that it is not all that bad.

The first thing you need to do before you know how to read a crochet pattern is to check the abbreviations used for all of the various stitches. You will use these symbols repeatedly when reading a pattern and you'll learn most of them easily. The table below includes a list of the most commonly used stitches and their abbreviations. You are going to learn more about these later on, but for now, you only need to read the abbreviations.

Common Crochet Terminology and Abbreviations

Terminology	Abbreviation
Chain	CH, ch
Single crochet	SC, sc
The half double crochet	HDC, hdc
The double crochet	DC, dc
The treble crochet	TR, tr
The double treble crochet	DTR, dtr
The extended single crochet	EXSC, exsc
The double treble crochet	DTR, dtr
Cluster	CL, cl
Group	GP, gp
Right side	RS
Slip stitch	Sl st, SS, ss
Space	sp
St(s)	Stitch(es)
Together	TOG, tog
Turning chain	tch
Wrong side	WS
Yarn over hook	yo

Asterisks, square brackets, and round brackets are used to simplify patterns.

Asterisks (*): An asterisk indicates that all the pattern information before it must be repeated until the end of that row.

Square Brackets [ ]: These are used to explain patterns that are complicated by placing additional information in the brackets.

Round Brackets (): Used for placing additional information in the brackets and also for indicating which stitches should be repeated. For example – (2ch) 9 times. This can be explained as 2 chain stitches to be repeated 9 times.

Something to keep in mind is that crochet terms differ in the UK and the US. This table will help you should you ever need this information.

Crochet Terms Used in UK and US

US	UK
The chain(ch)	The chain(ch)
The single crochet(sc)	The double crochet(dc)
The half double crochet(hdc)	The half treble(htr)
The double crochet(dc)	The treble(tr)
The treble crochet(trc)	The double treble crochet(dtr)

Make sure you pay attention to the terms used before purchasing patterns.

Reading crochet patterns can be fairly time-consuming at first, but you'll get used to it. Patterns are written in rows for items that are straight and flat, such as a square cloth. For something like a coaster, the pattern is written in rounds, this is the terminology we use.

Here is a row to practice reading - Row 1: Chain 12, dc in 2nd chain from the hook and across in each. Chain 1, turn (9)

Firstly, you can see that this is part of a pattern from a straight, flat item because the pattern refers to row 1. Next, chain 12 indicates that this is a chain made up of 12 chain stitches.

After this, there will be the half double crochet in chain number two from the hook (excluding the one carried by the hook). This is followed by the half double crochet in each stitch till the end of the row. Then you'll make one chain stitch for the following row.

Ready to try another one? This time we'll look at using asterisks. Here we'll focus on what part of the pattern needs to be repeated. Leave a piece of long thread, chain 21. Sc in the second chain and in each across. (20 sts) - approximately 5" wide

Row 1: *single crochet in first st, double crochet in the next* repeat till the end. Chain 1 and turn (20 stitches)

Leave a long piece of yarn, then start your chain which will be 21 stitches long. Next make a single crochet in the second Ch stitch from the hook is (exclude the stitch with is attached to the hook) and also single crochet in each chain until the end of the row. It should be approximately 10 inches wide.

In row one, read the pattern carefully. You'll notice that there are only two asterisks. Everything in between the asterisks needs to get repeated till where the row ends. Firstly, the single crochet is done in the first stitch, then the double crochet is what follows in the next. Then, a single crochet in the first stitch comes again and is then followed by the double crochet. Follow through till the row ends. Make 1 chain stitch so that you can begin a new row.

This is just one example; you will learn as you go along. In addition to reading written patterns, you will also be able to use symbols to read patterns. Below is an elaborate list of common crochet symbols that are commonly used.

Chapter 18 FAQ's About Yarn Care

Here is a quick roundup of the most common questions that are asked about how to best care for your yarn or wool.

Can You Wash An Entire Skein?

In some cases you may need to wash the skeins or yarn balls before use (spillages etc) and although this can be difficult it is possible. The trickiest part about this is to ensure that the yarn doesn't unravel which you can do by putting it in a pair of tights or washing bag beforehand. However, make sure to follow the same washing guidelines and check to see that all detergent has been rinsed out (you may need to hand rinse them to make sure as this could cause irritation if there is residue)

How Often Should You Wash Yarn Or Wool?

This depends on the amount of wear and the purpose of the project. For example a crochet bag may only need to be sponged down once in a while whereas clothes would need to be washed more frequently. Clothes such as socks would definitely need to be washed after each use to avoid any fungal or bacterial infections while a jumper may be worn a few times before needing to be washed. It entirely depends.

Can You Dye Your Own Yarn?

The answer to this is yes and the easiest types of yarn to dye are those that are animal fibers, for example alpaca, wool or mohair. Make sure to protect your skin and clothes when dying your own yarn as it easily transfers and can cause a large mess. For synthetic yarn you will need to buy specific dye to use for the fiber.

How Do You Find Yarn Care Instructions For Other Yarn?

Usually, yarn will come with a wraparound label that has specific washing instructions on the outside or overleaf of the label. Some special types of yarn will come with packet instructions and others may not come with anything at all. The more specialised the yarn is, the more likely you are to get instructions. Generally speaking worsted weight yarn which is most commonly used is also more durable which means you are less likely to get specific instructions.

Can You Get Rid Of Old Stains And Smells?

Yes, however not always and a lot of dried on stains or lingering smells are hard to get rid of. The longer the stain or smell has been present on the fiber, the harder it is to get rid of.

Can You Tumble Dry?

It is best not to tumble dry yarn or wool as it is very sensitive to temperature and it can make it rough or coarse on the skin (as well as risk of shrinking) if it is exposed to higher temperatures. If you choose to use the tumble dryer it is best to do so on a cool or very low heat setting for short amounts at a time to check it is not having adverse effects on the fibers.

How Long Can You Keep Yarn Or Wool For?

Wool or yarn can be kept for a very long time over a range of years if it is stored properly in the right conditions and maintained. Wool that has been kept for over 10 years may not be viable for crocheting or knitting because it has started to degrade but this depends on the type. Organic fibers that haven't been treated may not last as long as store-bought that have been chemically treated.

How Do You Store Yarn?

Store in skeins or balls in a dry place and make sure to clean out and check frequently to avoid your stash coming into contact with a lot of dust, moths or pests that might contaminate the supply. In addition avoid getting your stash wet and ensure that you frequently air it out to avoid there being a musty smell embedded in the yarn.

Conclusions

By now, I hope that you have grown to love the art of amigurumi as I have. These adorable stuffed creatures can be tailored to be created with any color of thread that you desire. Your imagination is the only limit.

These crafts make great gifts for people of all ages!

Take care and happy stitching!

CPSIA information can be obtained
at www.ICGtesting.com
Printed in the USA
BVHW041439010421
603931BV00007B/264